Cucina Closed

A cookbook featuring our Italian manufacturers
and their family recipes

Making cappelletti and ravioli? Easy! Claudia, Maria and Shanti show you how it's done (p. 100).

"We would like to share our love of Italian craftsmanship."

There is much more linking us to Italy than a passion for Italian food. Although we love the cuisine, that is not what originally drew us to this very special country. The story of our fashion brand began in a little workshop near Ancona more than 40 years ago, when the first Closed jeans were handcrafted. Some of the design elements used then can still be seen in our current collections. To this day, our jeans come from Italy.

Over the decades, we have had the privilege of getting to know the best weaving companies and laundries for denim in this stunning country. That's not all, though. We have also grown very fond of the special people who make our products there every single day. Whenever we visit them, food plays a crucial role. It is an essential part of Italian hospitality. Many of our production partners have become our friends. They always welcome us with open arms and tables full of food. Over the years, we have become increasingly aware of just how many similarities there are between preparing a meal and manufacturing high-quality fashion. Both combine traditional craftsmanship with carefully chosen ingredients and close attention to detail.

That is how we came up with the idea behind this cookbook. We want to share the family recipes that our Italian partners and friends love and, above all, introduce the special people behind the dishes. On our trips to Italy, we have visited their homes, cooked together, and shared food, drinks and laughter. We have also stopped off at lots of wonderful places with interesting culinary roots, learning how traditional pasta is made, watching pastry chefs at work, and much more.

All of our experiences come together in this book, which we hope will inspire you and bring a little of the dolce vita to your kitchen.

Buon appetito!

Gordon Giers

Maurizio's winery is home to a real treasure:
an old family castle, including a rustic kitchen (p. 148).

RUTTA
PANTO
SUCCI DANIELE

Az. Agr.
Molè
PRODOTTO: MELANZANA VIOLETTA - CAT. «II» - CAL. NO
RIUTILIZZO VIETATO
TARA GR 1500
ITALIA
Bontà di
ORTOFRUTTICOLA
F.lli CERRATO
A VISTA
COOPERATIVA LAVORATORI
Santa Marianna Soc. Coop.
DESCRIZIONE ED ORIGINE
VEDI ETICHETTA CONFEZIONE
SICILIA
SPAGNA

TASSO

The weekly farmers' market in Padua has over 190 stalls

As fresh as it gets: Fabrizio's grigliata di pesce (p. 156).

The most important rule when it comes to homemade pasta – get family or friends to help you!

Antipasti

Before the main courses hit the plates, it's time for some starters – from fried courgette flowers to vitello tonnato or bruschette

Alessandra and Carla's fried courgette flowers

Prep 1 h   Cook 20 min   Serves 4

15 g yeast

300 g flour

Salt, pepper

12 courgette flowers

125 g mozzarella, cut into 12 pieces

12 anchovies in oil (optional)

Peanut oil for frying

Stuffed and fried courgette flowers originated as finger food typical of Roman Jewish cuisine. At first, they were filled with mozzarella and anchovies. Today, mozzarella by itself or a ricotta cream are popular. "You should eat them while they're still hot," recommends Alessandra. "That's when they're at their crispiest."

Dissolve the yeast in 300 ml lukewarm water. Put the flour in a large bowl, add the yeast water little by little, mixing with a whisk until a uniform batter is formed. Season with salt and pepper to taste. Then cover the bowl with the batter with plastic wrap and leave to rest in the fridge for an hour.

In the meantime, carefully wash the courgette flowers. Open the flowers and gently remove the pistils and stems with a small knife. Then pat the flowers dry. Carefully fill each flower with a piece of mozzarella and an anchovy. Squeeze flowers gently to close them.

Heat plenty of peanut oil in a steel pan with high sides over high heat. Take the batter out of the fridge. Dip the first stuffed courgette flower into the batter and turn until it is completely covered (you may need to help with a spoon). Then place in the hot oil and deep-fry for 4–5 minutes until the batter is evenly browned. Do the same with the other flowers. Do not put too many in the pan at once so that the oil temperature does not drop.

Drain the fried flowers on some kitchen paper and serve immediately.

Alessandra and Carla's fried courgette flowers

To the table, everyone, please!
From left to right: Alessandra, her parents Carla and Giulio and her brother Enrico.

"When we sit down for a meal, we try not to talk too much about work."

Alessandra is the second generation to head the family business Cinturificio G&G. Her father Giulio founded the small workshop, which manufactures belts and leather accessories. Today, he still drops in from time to time, while Alessandra and her brother Enrico run the business. Their mother Carla makes sure everyone is well fed. "We eat together every day. There is no exception."

Fiori di zucca fritti – crispy, fried courgette flowers stuffed with mozzarella – are Alessandra's favourite food. "My mother makes them better than anyone else. She's mastered the art of closing the flowers so that none of the filling oozes out in the frying pan," she says. Alessandra adds that the secret is carefully twisting the fine petals together. You need a steady hand to do this, but that is pretty much a given in Alessandra's family.

In 1983, Alessandra's father Giulio established a small workshop manufacturing leather goods. Called Cinturificio G&G, it can be found in the village of Saletto di Vigodarzere near Padua. Closed has its belts made there. Cinturificio G&G is a family business through and through. Giulio's wife joined the company in 1993. The couple's children, Alessandra and Enrico, grew up in the workshop. "We helped out from an early age," says Alessandra.

Now, they have taken the reins. Although Alessandra and Enrico keep an eye on everything, they each have their own specific responsibilities. "I'm an administrator – I deal with suppliers, procurement, clients, samples, production, invoicing and payment runs," says Alessandra. "My brother has more to do with the workshop. He gets the machines ready for processing the leather, uses them to cut belts, and attaches studs and buckles." Their parents are gradually retiring from the business. Giulio still pops in regularly and helps out. Carla makes lunch for the family on weekdays. "We eat together every day without exception," comments Alessandra. "And we try not to talk about work over lunch."

That is most likely to succeed if there's a big plate of fiori di zucca fritti on the table. "The dish is in season in spring," says Alessandra. "As a starter, it goes well with risotto with asparagus (p. 90)." These stuffed courgette flowers also make a good main course, however. For best results, you need to make sure that the oil used to fry them is neither too hot nor too cold – 180 to 190 degrees is perfect. "Mum turns them a few times using a fork to make sure they cook evenly," adds Alessandra. "They're perfect with a glass of ice-cold prosecco."

Luana's polenta flatbreads

Prep 15 min Cook 5 min Serves 4

450 g polenta, cooked (e.g. a leftover from the day before)

2 tbsp olive oil

250–300 g flour (type 405)

Salt, pepper

Salami, ham, cheese to taste

Flatbreads are typical of the small municipality of Urbania in the Marche. Tradition has it that they are always prepared when there is polenta left over from the day before. They are eaten with salami, ham and cheese. "It's a dish that also introduces children to cooking because it's so simple," says Luana.

Put the polenta in a bowl with the olive oil. Gradually stir in the flour. It should form a smooth, even dough. Add salt and pepper to taste.

Roll out 12 small patties from the dough with a rolling pin, about 2 mm thick.

In a hot pan without oil, fry flatbreads for 30–40 seconds on both sides.

Traditionally, polenta flatbreads are served with salami, ham and cheese. They are also delicious when filled with lettuce and tomatoes.

Luana's polenta flatbreads

At the weekly market of Porto San Giorgio, a small harbour community south of Ancona.

PASTA ALL'UOVO
€ 2,90
CONF

Carlo's passatina with bacon and shrimps

Prep 25 min Cook 2 h* Serves 4

1 onion, finely chopped

1 carrot, cut into 1 cm pieces

1 stick of celery, cut into 1 cm pieces

5 tbsp olive oil

200 g chickpeas, soaked in water for 12–24 hours*

2 sprigs rosemary, leaves plucked off and chopped

1 potato, cut into 1 cm cubes

Salt, pepper

80 g lardo (Italian pork bacon), finely diced

12 shrimps (dearmed)

1 garlic clove, finely chopped

A passatina is a purée with a very runny consistency. A version of this chickpea dish topped with shrimps was made world-famous by the celebrity chef Fulvio Pierangelini. Now, there are more and more different variations of the dish. "I like to add bacon," says Carlo.

In a non-stick pan, sauté the onions, carrots and celery with 2 tbsp. olive oil. Add the chickpeas and half the rosemary leaves, cover with water.

Add the potato. Simmer gently over a low heat for 2 hours, stirring occasionally so that nothing burns. If necessary, add a little more water.

Remove the pot from the heat. Using a hand blender, mash everything until it is a smooth purée. Salt and pepper to taste.

Fry the prawns with 3 tbsp olive oil on both sides for 2–3 minutes until cooked. Season with salt and pepper to taste.

Mix the lardo with the garlic and remaining rosemary. Pepper to taste. Spread the lardo on plates and place the hot passatina on top. Serve with a little olive oil and the fried prawns as a topping.

*For ready-cooked canned chickpeas, the cooking time is only about 20 minutes.

Carlo's passatina with bacon and shrimps

"Food and fashion must be made with love – and by hand."

Carlo is the manager of the denim laundry Green Lab. He took over the business from his father. Originally, he wanted to cook – and even started an Italian restaurant with friends in Copenhagen. "The hype quickly became a bit too much for me. So I went into the family business."

"It's important to soak the chickpeas for a long time," says Carlo. The preparations for his chickpea passatina with bacon and shrimps should ideally start the day before it is served. "The water has to be changed at least twice during that time." Chickpeas contain the toxin phasin, but soaking them gets rid of this. (If short on time, tinned chickpeas can be used instead.)

Carlo is the Managing Director of Green Lab, a denim laundry that washes and finishes jeans for Closed with the smallest possible environmental impact. "We're constantly working on new ideas and processes to become eco-friendlier." Green Lab is based in the village of Grottammare, about 80 kilometres south of Ancona. The company is now under third-generation management. "My grandfather came from Florence. He started dyeing textiles there, then moved here to the Marche region," says Carlo. "My father turned the dyeing business into a laundry where consumers could bring their things. The 1980s brought a denim boom and we started washing jeans then. At first, we did that with conventional machines." Now, Green Lab has around 44 members of staff. "Quite a few of them, like Fabrizio (p. 158), have known me since I was born."

Carlo never planned to take over the family business. "I always wanted to cook," he says. With that goal in mind, he concentrated on it even at school. "I loved giving old recipes a modern twist and making vegetarian versions of classic meat dishes." His cannelloni with a ricotta and lemon filling (p. 142) are a particular speciality. When he finished school, Carlo moved to Copenhagen and opened a restaurant with a few friends. "At first, it was just a pop-up." Now, Mangia is one of the best-known Italian restaurants in the Danish capital. "The hype surrounding it soon became too much for me, so I came back to Italy and joined the family business." That was in 2016.

Now, he only cooks for pleasure. To make his chickpea passatina, Carlo cuts celery, onions and carrots into small pieces and fries them lightly. He drains the chickpeas well and adds them, along with a potato. This mixture is cooked on a low heat for two hours. The golden rule is only to add seasoning right at the end once the chickpeas are soft. "Salt stops them from cooking properly," he says. Last but not least, Carlo uses a hand blender to purée the mixture.

What makes Carlo's passatina really special is its filling and topping. He puts finely cut raw lardo (a famous white, fatty bacon made in Italy) with rosemary and garlic at the bottom of a bowl, then spreads the hot chickpea purée over it. "That causes the bacon to start melting and release its flavour." Next, Carlo sears shrimps and arranges them on the passatina. The result is a layered antipasti. "Scoop your spoon right the way through for a taste sensation!"

ENGRAULES ENCRASICOLUS
ALICI
ACQUA DOLCE
ACQUACOLTURA
PESCATO
ALLEVATO
DECONGELATO
€ 10
PROVENIENZA
MEDITERRANEO
ATLANTICO NORD OCCIDENTALE
ATLANTICO NORD ORIENTALE
ATLANTICO CENTRO OCCIDENTALE
ATLANTICO CENTRO ORIENTALE
ATLANTICO SUD OCCIDENTALE
ATLANTICO SUD ORIENTALE
ADRIATICO
MAR BALTICO
MARE DEL NORD
MARE NERO
OCEANO INDIANO
OCEANO PACIFICO
ANTARTICO

In addition to freshly caught fish such as anchovies, you can find handmade pasta at the Porto San Giorgio weekly market.

Claudia's vitello tonnato

Prep 1 h Cook 25 min Serves 6

For the vitello:

3 tbsp olive oil + more to drizzle

1 onion, finely chopped

1 carrot, cut into 1 cm pieces

1 stick of celery, cut into 1 cm pieces

800 g veal loin

Salt, pepper

50 ml dry white wine

For the salsa tonnata:

300 g tuna in oil (preferably in a jar), drained

30 g anchovies in oil

20 g capers + more for the decoration

100 g mayonnaise

2–3 stems of parsley

This appetiser first appeared in recipe books in the 19th century. Originally, the sauce was made with anchovies and capers. Only later did tuna become an ingredient for the sauce. "My recipe dates back to the eighties," says Claudia. "But it still tastes fantastic."

In a non-stick pan, sauté the onions, carrots and celery with 2 tbsp olive oil. Add the boiled veal in one piece, salt and fry until light brown on all sides.

Add the wine and 2 l water. Season with salt and pepper to taste. Simmer for approx. 1 hour, turning the meat from time to time. Then remove and leave to cool.

In the meantime, prepare the salsa tonnata. Blitz the tuna, anchovies, capers and 1–2 sprigs of parsley in a blender or with a hand blender until you have a smooth, creamy sauce with a slightly runny consistency. Dilute with water if necessary. Season with salt and pepper to taste.

Cut the cooled meat into very thin slices. Pluck off the remaining parsley leaves.

Lay out the veal slices on a serving plate and cover evenly with salsa tonnata. Decorate with capers, parsley leaves and a drizzle of olive oil.

Silvia's crostini with radicchio

Prep 15 min Cook 15 min Serves 4

3 tbsp olive oil

1 large red onion, finely sliced

75 g smoked bacon, cut into fine strips (optional)

½ tsp chilli flakes

1 radicchio (approx. 150 g), cut into fine strips

1 tsp honey

Salt, pepper

6 slices of farmhouse bread

30 g Pecorino cheese, grated

The story behind crostini is a typical Tuscan one. In rural and poorer parts of Tuscany, bread was always put on the table to mop up any leftover sauce, which people didn't want to waste. Over the centuries, this habit gave rise to today's antipasti, whereby slices of bread are toasted and topped with a variety of ingredients. "The radicchio version also goes wonderfully with a BBQ," says Silvia.

Silvia's crostini with radicchio

Heat 2 tbsp olive oil in a frying pan. Add the onions, bacon and chilli flakes and stir-fry over a medium heat. Then add the radicchio strips and sauté until they collapse. Stir in the honey. Season with salt and pepper to taste.

Cut the bread slices in half and roast in the oven at 180 degrees for about 12 minutes until lightly browned. Mix the radicchio with the remaining oil and spread evenly over the bread. Serve sprinkled with Pecorino cheese.

"Nobody likes to eat in a hurry. When I'm cooking, I also like to take my time."

Silvia takes care of communication with partners at Pooltrend, a manufacturer of knitted accessories. "I've always been in the textile industry. I can't imagine anything else," she says. Crostini with radicchio have also been with her all her life. "My mother used to prepare them."

"The best way to cut up the radicchio is to use a mezzaluna knife," says Silvia. Typically, she will pile up the slightly bitter salad leaves on a chopping board in front of her, before going over them a few times with the knife until she has cut them into pieces two to three centimetres long. "That's the perfect size for crostini," she says. This dish is a traditional starter or quick snack.

Silvia works at Pooltrend, which specialises in knitted accessories. The business is located in the town of Montemurlo, which belongs to the province of Prato. Closed sources products like high-quality scarves and blankets from Pooltrend. Silvia has been a member of the commercial team there since 2021. With her colleagues Lorenzo (p. 178) and Barbara (p. 124), she is responsible for liaising with partners and ensuring that their collaboration goes smoothly. "I've always worked in the textile industry and can't really imagine doing anything else," she says.

Crostini with radicchio is a dish that has been served throughout Silvia's life. "My mother used to prepare it and showed me how it's done. Now, I like making it for my husband and children."

Crostini can be served as a starter, snack or side dish. "The bitter-sweet flavour of the sautéed leaves goes well with meat, so I often serve crostini when we have a barbecue in the garden, too." Radicchio is usually eaten in spring and summer, when it is in season.

For the crostini topping, the chopped leaves have to be fried on a low heat with olive oil, salt and pepper for about ten minutes. "The salad should be slightly wilted but still have a bit of crunch," she adds. Meanwhile, she toasts the slices of bread in the oven. Last but not least, she arranges the radicchio on the bread, drizzles a little olive oil over everything and grates creamy Pecorino cheese finely on top. "That rounds off the flavour of the radicchio perfectly."

Silvia's crostini with radicchio

Andrea's frittata with peas

Prep 10 min Cook 5 min Serves 4

30 g butter

150 g shallots, finely chopped

8 eggs

Salt, pepper

125 ml milk

250 g peas (fresh or frozen), cooked

40 g Parmesan cheese, grated

Frittata is the Italian omelette. The difference between the two egg dishes is that the frittata's setting egg mixture is turned over while cooking in the pan and not served folded. In the past, the idea of the dish was to use up leftovers from previous days. Today it is a popular and quick snack. "It only takes a few minutes to prepare. È semplice!" says Andrea.

Melt the butter in a non-stick frying pan. Fry the shallots over a medium heat until translucent brown.

Meanwhile, beat the eggs in a bowl. Salt and pepper to taste.

Add milk and sautéed shallots to eggs and whisk. Pour the egg mixture into the pan. Spread peas on top and fry frittata over low to medium heat. As soon as the eggs are set, place a large plate on the pan and carefully turn the frittata over.

Fry for a few minutes on the other side.

Sprinkle Parmesan over the frittata before serving. Serve with a wild herb salad.

"When you work a lot, food has to taste especially good."

Andrea works in the sales department of the denim laundry Everest. That's why he's often on the road – and doesn't always have a lot of time to cook. "But frittata is always doable," he says. He learned the recipe for the egg dish from his mother.

To make the frittata creamy, Andrea adds the milk when the egg is still runny.

"The peas are the only time-consuming bit, but even they don't take long," says Andrea. Before they can be used as a filling for his frittata, they need to be shelled and cooked – either briefly in boiling, salted water or with a little oil in a non-stick pan. Andrea recommends the second method: "I add bacon for extra flavour. Everything else is ready in no time at all."

Frittata with peas is Andrea's signature dish. "It was the first thing my mother taught me to make. Then came pizza and risotto," he says. When he was a little boy, he wanted to be a chef, and he practised in the kitchen at home whenever he could. "As is so often the case, I chose a completely different profession in the end though."

Andrea is a member of the sales team at Everest, a denim laundry which washes and finishes jeans for Closed. It is located on the outskirts of a small town called Piombino Dese, about 40 kilometres north-west of Venice. Andrea's job is presenting new products and innovations to brands and designers regularly. "I explain what we do and how we can adapt the products for their collections." Sometimes clients come to the showroom, and sometimes he visits them. People who travel a lot don't usually have much time for cooking. But, as Andrea likes to say, "There's always time for a frittata."

Simply whisk the eggs while braising the red onions. Then put the eggs in the pan, add the peas and bacon, and sprinkle in Parmesan, salt and pepper. Cook it on a low heat. Is that it? Andrea has another trick up his sleeve: add some milk when everything is in the pan and the egg is still runny. "That makes the frittata extra creamy," he says. You can fill it with anything you like. "Just yesterday, I substituted the peas with tomatoes, bacon and Val Pusteria mountain cheese."

Lush meadows, deep forests: south-west of Padua lies the Euganean Hills Regional Park. Its microclimate produces excellent olive oil and wild fruits.

Rosanna's fried mozzarella cheese balls

Prep 30 min Cook 15 min Serves 4

2 eggs

Salt, pepper

80 g flour

150 g breadcrumbs

250 g mozzarella,
cut into 2–3 cm pieces

Oil for frying

Delicious, melting mozzarella has been served in crispy bread since the 18th century. La mozzarella in carrozza is what you might call Italy's answer to a cheese sandwich. Fried mozzarella cheese balls (or mozzarelline impanate) are the finger-food version. "Eat them while they're still hot," says Rosanna.

Crack the eggs into a shallow bowl. Season with salt and pepper to taste. Whisk well. Put the flour and breadcrumbs in two other shallow bowls. Season with salt and pepper.

First turn the mozzarella pieces in the flour until they are evenly coated. Lightly roll into balls between your hands, carefully tapping off any excess flour. Then dip the mozzarella pieces into the beaten eggs and immediately turn them in the breadcrumbs until they are evenly coated on all sides. Dip the breaded balls into the eggs one more time and then turn them again in the breadcrumbs. The double breading makes the coating particularly crispy. Carefully place the breaded balls on a plate without stacking them.

Heat the oil in a frying pan with high sides. Once the oil is hot, deep-fry the mozzarella balls. The oil must not get too hot or the mozzarella will melt too quickly. Turn the balls often with a fork until they are evenly golden brown. Carefully lift out of the pan with a spoon and drain on kitchen paper. Serve with a drizzle of tomato sauce.

Rosanna's fried mozzarella cheese balls

"I enjoy the process of creating something from scratch."

Rosanna works at the Paul denim sewing shop. She specialises in trousers, the seams on the waistband in particular. She has been perfecting the craft since her school days. "I also like to cook with my hands and do everything myself," she says. "You can see right away what you have accomplished."

Anyone can make Rosanna's mozzarelline impanate, and everyone loves them. Mozzarelline are quite simply little balls of mozzarella cheese. "Impanate" means breaded. "You can often buy them ready-made, but I prefer to make them from scratch myself. You can immediately see what you have accomplished," she says.

Rosanna has a similar philosophy at work. Ever since she left school, she has worked in trouser manufacturing. She likes to make things on her own. She took a job at Paul in 1992. The company is based in Ostra, a small town about 50 kilometres north-west of Ancona. Closed has its jeans sewn there. Rosanna specialises in the seams on the waistband. She could have retired a long time ago, but she still works part-time. "What would I do all day?" she asks. "There's nothing to do at home, and the people at work are nice."

She coats mozzarella cheese balls in flour, then dips them in egg and covers them with breadcrumbs to make a classic breadcrumb coating. It's important to cover the mozzarella thoroughly and firmly so that the coating doesn't split in the frying pan, allowing the cheese to ooze out. The oil shouldn't be too hot for the same reason. "When you put the balls in the oil, it should sizzle, but the oil shouldn't be bubbling. I turn each ball several times with a fork until it's golden brown."

Once they are cooked, leave the mozzarella cheese balls on a piece of kitchen roll to drain off excess oil and allow them to cool. "They taste best warm," advises Rosanna.

Rosanna's fried mozzarella cheese balls

CLEMENTINE
PERE
MELE GOLD
ARANCE
AGRIFONDO
AGRIFONDO

PEPERONI
POMODORO MERINDA
COSTE
Mercato di Piazza
Banco n
Paolo
Arcimboldo

Claudia's bruschette

Prep 1 h Cook 30 min Serves 4

1 ciabatta (or white loaf), cut into slices

1 red onion, finely sliced

1 tbsp balsamic vinegar

Salt, pepper

1 small bunch of parsley, finely chopped

1 garlic clove, finely chopped

2 tbsp olive oil

120 g cherry tomatoes, quartered

½ peperoncino, finely chopped (alternatively ½ tsp chilli flakes)

1 handful of basil leaves, torn

2 salsiccia (Italian sausages, pressed out of their skins)

2 tbsp cream cheese

"Bruscare" means as much as toast in Italian. Bruschette were originally slices of stale bread that were grilled then topped with whatever was to hand. It was a poor people's meal. Today, it is an appetiser that can be quickly prepared. "Never toast the bread in a frying pan: put it in the oven! That way you don't run the risk of it burning," says Claudia.

Toast the bread slices in the oven at 180 degrees for about 12 minutes until lightly browned. Marinate the onion strips in a bowl with balsamic vinegar. Season with salt and pepper to taste. Spread evenly on a quarter of the bread slices.

Mix the parsley and garlic with 1 tbsp olive oil. Season with salt and pepper to taste. Leave to marinate for approx. ½ hour, then spread evenly over a quarter of the bread slices.

Mix the cherry tomatoes, 1 tbsp olive oil, chilli pepper and basil together. Season with salt and pepper to taste. Marinate for ½ hour and spread evenly on a quarter of the bread slices.

Mix the salsiccia with the cream cheese. Season with salt and pepper to taste. Spread evenly on a quarter of the bread slices. Grill in the oven at 200 degrees for about 15 minutes. Serve warm.

Pastificio Irma

Pasta e basta!

Giovanni studied European business, but then took over a traditional pasta-making factory in Milan. Today, Pastificio Irma is one of the best small food businesses in the city.

At the end of a narrow shopping arcade just around the corner from Milan's Piazza Piemonte is a little pasta paradise by the name of Pastificio Irma. The counter is packed with fresh tagliatelle, bigoli, fusilli, gnocchi and all sorts of other types of pasta. Next to it is a large table where everything is made and in front of the counter are three tables with six bar stools. If you want to, you can take a seat in the shop and watch the pasta makers at work. There is also a small lunch menu. "We're always pleased when someone wants to see the work that goes into making good pasta," says Giovanni.

Giovanni is the owner of Pastificio Irma. (Irma was the woman who founded it in 1959.) Giovanni took over the company in 2019 because he loves pasta so much. He studied European business and taught himself the art of pasta making – how to achieve the perfect balance of flour, egg and water, how to knead the dough and let it rest. "I'm self-taught, but I'm always on the lookout for the best ingredients and recipes," he says.

Pastificio Irma doesn't just sell plain fresh pasta. It specialises in filled pasta – recipes from the whole of Italy, some of which had fallen into oblivion. There are little cappelletti, for example, which are typical of the Marche region and Emilia-Romagna, filled with ricotta, saffron and lemon or artichoke and pepper. Culurgiones are also a highlight of the product range. These long pasta parcels from Sardinia are stuffed with potato, truffle and Pecorino, then pinched so artistically that they look braided. "It took ages for me to master that," comments Giovanni. "But that was the point."

For him, pasta isn't just a culinary treat. It is also a culture stretching back hundreds or even thousands of years. "I don't want everything to be forgotten," he says. His customers seem to appreciate it. The business is doing so well that Giovanni has started a delivery service, which is increasingly popular with older customers in particular. He employs six people: three pasta makers and three cooks who make the fillings plus sauces to take away, like a Bolognese sauce.

Does he still want to cook for himself after all that pasta making? "Always," says Giovanni. His favourite pasta is fusilli al ferretto. "It originally comes from Calabria and has an extra long corkscrew shape which means that it holds a lot of sauce." It goes without saying that this is also among the products for sale at Pastificio Irma.

MESTIERE, PATRIMONIO DI
QUELLO CHE SIAMO E SAREMO.
GRANO DURO
GRANO DURO SEMINTEGRALE
PANE
LIEVITO
MADRE
CASSETTA SEMINTEGRALE
BACCALÁ
RICOTTA & SPINACI

Giovanni has now mastered the craft of pasta making to perfection. He learned it all by himself.

FATTA A MANO

Pastificio Irma produces classic types of pasta like linguine (right page), but also rare varieties like culurgiones (this page).

Primi

It's time for the first main course – and fortunately in Italy that often means pasta! In addition to cappelletti and lasagne, risotto or crespelle are served

Antonio's sagne e fagioli

Prep 45 min   Cook 40 min   Serves 4

400 g durum wheat flour

Salt, pepper

2 tbsp olive oil + a little more for drizzling

½ onion, finely chopped

1 stick of celery, finely chopped

1 carrot, finely chopped

2 tbsp tomato purée

250 g borlotti beans (soaked overnight in water, alternatively 2 cans of borlotti beans, drained weight 240 g each)

400 g chopped tomatoes (tinned)

150 g bacon, finely diced

½ tsp chilli flakes

This traditional pasta dish from the Abruzzo region is considered a fortifying meal. Legend has it that it was once primarily cooked for nursing mothers. Now, almost every family in the region has its own special recipe. "I like to add bacon," says Antonio.

Mix the flour with a pinch of salt and add approx. 200 ml lukewarm water to make a smooth, even dough. Then knead the dough, cover with foil and leave to rest for about 30 minutes. Roll out the dough to a thickness of approx. 2 mm using a rolling pin or pasta machine. Then cut into noodles about 1 cm wide and 5 cm long. Dust with a little flour and leave to rest.

Heat the olive oil in a pot. Add the onions, carrot and celery. Stir-fry for about 5 minutes. Stir in the tomato purée and fry briefly. Add the beans with 1.5 l water and the tomatoes. Salt and pepper to taste. Cook for 30 minutes over medium heat, adding a little water if necessary.

Fry the bacon at a high temperature in a pan without oil until crispy. Remove and set aside.

In the meantime, boil the pasta in salted water until al dente. Add the cooked pasta and the bacon to the beans in the pot and mix everything together. Serve with a little olive oil and chilli flakes to taste.

Antonio's sagne e fagioli

"I know all my favourite recipes from my childhood."

Antonio is the General Manager of the denim sewing company Incom. He supervises all the work steps to ensure that everything runs smoothly. Logically, he also makes the pasta for his sagne e fagioli himself. He has known the dish since he was a little boy. "I remember my grandparents cooking it by the fireplace."

Sagne e fagioli means "pasta and beans". This dish tastes much more interesting than it might sound. It is served with a sauce made from sun-ripened tomatoes, creamy borlotti beans and a hint of chilli. The pasta is what makes this dish special. Sagne is a kind of short tagliatelle which is very easy to pick up with a fork. "It's about two millimetres thick, one centimetre wide and five centimetres long," says Antonio. He prides himself on making the pasta himself.

Antonio is the General Manager at Incom, which is based in the town of Urbania, about a 90-minute drive west of Ancona. This highly innovative firm carefully hand-stitches jeans and denim jackets for Closed. Antonio has been working there since 2018. He is responsible for the smooth running of the whole company, from HR and finance to sample production, manufacturing, procurement and logistics. This means it's important for him to have a good relationship with his colleagues. It's not unusual for him to meet co-workers like Claudio (p. 74) socially. "It's more than just a job to me," he says. "It's a vocation. My family instilled the necessary sense of responsibility in me when I was a child." His love of sagne e fagioli stems from his childhood, too.

The dish originally comes from the Abruzzo region east of Rome. Antonio grew up there. "In winter, we ate it at least once a week. I remember my grandparents cooking it by the fire," he says. To follow the original recipe, it's important to soak the dried beans in water the evening before making the dish (alternatively, you can skip this step by using tinned beans). "The next morning, you rinse the beans and put them in water again for an hour with a few bay leaves." This enhances the flavour. For even more of a taste sensation, he adds, "Just keep the water and use it to cook the sauce and pasta."

To make the sauce, Antonio browns finely chopped carrots, celery and onions in a pan before adding the beans and chopped tomatoes. The mixture is then left to simmer for approximately 30 minutes. In the meantime, he boils the sagne. As soon as it is cooked al dente, he adds it to the beans. "I put in a little olive oil and chilli, then leave the mixture to rest for two minutes. That allows the pasta to absorb the sauce and gives it a fuller flavour." Then all that is needed is the right wine. Antonio recommends a Montepulciano – from the Abruzzo region, naturally. "A bottle of La Botte di Gianni from Masciarelli winery is the perfect choice."

They like to work and eat together:
Claudio (left) and Antonio (right).

POLO

Claudio's filled gnocchi

Prep 45 min
Cook 30 min
Serves 4–6

For the potato dough:

500 g potatoes, boiled and peeled

300 g flour

1 egg + 1 egg yolk, beaten

5 tbsp olive oil

Salt, pepper

For the vegetable filling:

2 tbsp olive oil

3 stems of chard, cut into 4–5 cm pieces

100 g spinach, fresh (or 70 g frozen), chopped

1 courgette, cut into 2–3 cm pieces

1 carrot, cut into 1–2 cm pieces

1 stick of celery, cut into 1–2 cm pieces

1 onion, finely chopped

For the béchamel sauce:

100 g butter

100 g flour

1 l fresh whole milk

Nutmeg, grated

20 g Pecorino or Parmesan cheese, grated

Originally, filled gnocchi were stuffed with a minced meat mixture. Today, vegetable fillings are just as popular. Claudio's version is special: instead of dumplings, he makes a roll of dough, which he then cuts into slices. "It goes well with a glass of ice-cold Bianchello del Metauro."

For the potato dough, finely mash the still hot potatoes with a potato masher. Mix with flour, eggs and olive oil. Season with salt and pepper to taste. Knead the dough. Leave to rest for approx. 30 minutes.

For the vegetable filling, heat the olive oil in a pan. Sauté the vegetables over a medium heat for 10 minutes. Season with salt and pepper to taste. Leave to cool.

For the béchamel sauce, melt the butter in a saucepan. Add the flour and stir for one minute over a very low heat. Pour in the milk, stirring carefully, taking care not to let it boil too much. Once it's boiling, cook for a further 10 minutes, stirring constantly to allow the sauce to thicken. Season with salt and pepper to taste, add a pinch of nutmeg.

Preheat the oven to 180 °C. Roll out the dough on a lightly floured work surface into an approx. 30 × 20 cm rectangle (approx. 5 mm thick). Spread the cooled vegetables on the lower third of it. Roll up the dough. Cut the resulting dough roll into slices about 2 cm thick. Layer the slices like a fan in a baking dish.

Continue working the dough until it is all used up. Spread the béchamel sauce over the gnocchi slices. Sprinkle with cheese. Bake in the oven at 180 °C for 20–30 minutes.

"Enjoy food, enjoy life. The rest will come naturally."

Claudio is in charge of the technical side of things at the Incom denim sewing company, making sure the machines are running and everything is safe. "Whether I'm at work or in the kitchen, my dog Jeep is always with me," he says.

"You can use all kinds of vegetables for the filling," says Claudio. His gnocchi are full of beet greens, spinach, courgette, carrot, celery and onion. "It has a good balance of bitter and sweeter flavours. You only achieve that by chopping all of the ingredients very finely though."

Claudio works at Incom, which sews jeans and denim jackets for Closed. The company draws on craftsmanship and innovativeness, and is based in the town of Urbania, about a 90-minute drive west of Ancona. Claudio has been working as a mechanic there since 2019. "I look after the whole technical side of things and make sure all the sewing machines are working and safe." It may sound like a lot of responsibility but, he says, "Not for me. I've been taking things apart and putting them together since I was a little boy." One of his first projects was his father's tractor. "Every day, I took parts out and put them back in again."

When he left school, he started his own business. Whenever a machine stopped working somewhere, Claudio would be called out. Even then, some of his clients were from the textile industry. "Adidas, Barbour, Puma. Sometimes they would fly me out to Germany or Morocco because no one else knew how to get a machine going." There came a point where the job got too much for him. "I'm very lucky to work at Incom now. I still like fixing things." Including his faithful dog, Jeep.

"I rescued him when he was seven months old," says Claudio. Jeep's original owners couldn't cope with him. "I thought: I'll sort him out. I taught him to find truffles. Now, Jeep is my most loyal companion." While Claudio is preparing his gnocchi, Jeep sits calmly and patiently by his side.

Once the vegetables have been fried lightly and left to cool, Claudio takes the gnocchi dough out of the fridge and rolls it out until it is about 30 centimetres wide and three or four millimetres thick. He adds a strip of vegetables about seven to eight centimetres wide, then rolls the dough up from the bottom to the top. "Next, I cut it into slices two to three centimetres thick, which I put in an oven dish." This means the filling of his gnocchi is visible from the outside, but it is also possible to make classic dumpling shapes instead and fill them. Last but not least, Claudio pours béchamel sauce over the gnocchi, grates cheese on top, and puts it all in the oven for about 20 to 30 minutes. "A Bianchello del Metauro complements it perfectly. That's a local white wine with a fruity bouquet."

Lidia and Luca's spaghetti alla carbonara

Prep 15 min Cook 10 min Serves 4

320 g spaghetti

Salt, pepper

200 g guanciale (bacon), finely diced

6 egg yolks*

70 g Pecorino, finely grated

*The leftover egg white is perfect for spumini, see p. 218 (Dolci).

Legend has it that this dish was originally made by coal merchants ("carbonari"), who are said to have cooked penne with bacon and grated cheese during their lunch breaks. Historians also support the theory that American soldiers stationed in Rome during the Second World War made a contribution towards the dish by asking Italians to cook something using their daily rations of eggs and bacon. No one knows its true origins, but one thing is certain: "This flavourful, creamy dish should not contain any cream," says Lidia.

Lidia and Luca's spaghetti alla carbonara

Put the spaghetti in boiling salted water and cook until al dente. Meanwhile, sauté the guanciale on medium heat in a large frying pan. The fat should come out, but the pieces should not become completely crispy.

In a bowl, mix the egg yolk with the grated Pecorino and some black pepper.

Drain the pasta, reserving the pasta water. Add the pasta to the pan with guanciale. Add egg-Pecorino mixture, stirring quickly and stirring in some pasta water. The sauce should become creamy but not too runny.

Lidia and Luca's spaghetti alla carbonara

"Cooking together is just as much fun as eating together."

Lidia is responsible for the creation of new collections at the denim sewing company Incom. Her son Luca works there from time to time as a fitting model. The two are also a well-coordinated team in the kitchen. "Spaghetti alla carbonara is one of our favourite dishes," she says.

"We make a great team in the kitchen," says Lidia, of her and her son Luca, who cook together whenever they find time. Lockdown gave Luca, who lives with Lidia, the opportunity to perfect his culinary skills. "Spaghetti alla carbonara became one of our favourite dishes."

Lidia works at Incom, which sews denim jackets and jeans for Closed with exceptional attention to detail. The company is based in the town of Urbania, about a 90-minute drive west of Ancona. Lidia is director of the collection department. She oversees the creation of each new collection, communicates with clients and partners, and checks whether all of the designs drape and fit how they're supposed to once they're finished.

"I've been doing this job since 2016 and I love it. Occasionally, Luca has come in to work for us as a fitting model so that we can see what the garments look like on," she says. Luca is currently studying sports science.

For their carbonara, Lidia and Luca use guanciale, a fatty, air-dried bacon prepared from pork jowl. Although this is traditionally used, it can be substituted with other types of bacon. "It's best to put it in a cold frying pan then turn on the hob. That allows it to render down really slowly."

In the meantime, they make the sauce by mixing egg yolk and Pecorino. "You can use the leftover egg white for something else. I usually make a dessert called spumini (p. 218)," says Lidia. The finely grated cheese is stirred into the whisked egg yolks until the mixture is stiff. "Then you can cook the spaghetti." As soon as it is cooked al dente, Luca takes it out of the pan using a pair of spaghetti tongs. He puts the dripping wet spaghetti straight into the frying pan with the bacon. "Now you add the mixture of egg and cheese. Season to taste with black pepper and stir well."

Lidia has a tip if the sauce is too thick. "Just add a bit of the water you used to boil the pasta. That will loosen it up."

Onelia's lasagne

Prep 50 min Cook 40 min Serves 4–6

For the Bolognese sauce:

2 tbsp olive oil

1 red onion, finely diced

1 clove of garlic, finely chopped

200 g carrots, cut into 1–2 cm pieces

200 g celeriac, cut into 1–2 cm pieces

500 g minced meat (mixed)

Salt, pepper

1 tbsp tomato purée

100 ml red wine

2 tins of tomatoes (chopped)

1 bay leaf

1 bunch oregano, leaves plucked off and finely chopped

1 pinch of sugar

For the béchamel sauce:

100 g butter

100 g flour

1 l fresh whole milk

Nutmeg, grated

8 fresh lasagne sheets (refrigerated)

20 g Parmesan cheese, grated

Even the ancient Romans made flat sheets of dough, which were then processed into strips, cooked and called lagana. This gave rise to today's lasagne. "The dish brings out the pure harmony between the people who come together at the same table to eat it," says Onelia.

Onelia's lasagne sheets are home-made, of course. Each layer is cooked separately so that the thin dough doesn't break.

For the Bolognese sauce, heat 1 tbsp olive oil in a large frying pan. Fry the vegetables over a medium heat for 10 minutes. Remove the vegetables, set aside. Add remaining oil to pan. Add minced meat and fry over high heat until brown. Season with salt and pepper to taste.

Add tomato purée, stir in and fry for 2 minutes more. Pour in red wine, cook over high heat for 5 minutes. Add roasted vegetables, tomatoes and bay leaf. Cook for 15 minutes over medium heat. Add oregano and season sauce with salt, pepper and sugar to taste.

For the béchamel sauce, melt the butter in a saucepan. Add the flour and stir for one minute over a very low heat. Pour in the milk, stirring carefully, taking care not to let it boil too much. Once it reaches the boiling stage, cook for a further 10 minutes, stirring constantly to allow the sauce to thicken. Season with salt and pepper to taste, add a pinch of nutmeg.

Preheat the oven to 200 °C (top/bottom heat).

Spread a small ladle of Bolognese sauce on the bottom of the baking dish and cover with lasagne sheets. Spread the Bolognese sauce on the lasagne sheets, cover with a thin layer of béchamel sauce. Continue in this way until both sauces have been used up. Finish with a layer of béchamel sauce and sprinkle cheese evenly on top.

Bake in the preheated oven on the middle shelf for about 30–40 minutes until the surface is browned.

"Cooking is a balance from work for me. I relax in the kitchen."

At the denim sewing shop Paul, Onelia is responsible for everything that happens before a pair of jeans is manufactured in serial production. She creates the samples, ensuring that everything fits well in the end. Since 1978, she has been working at the company. "I've been making my lasagne for at least that long, too."

"Fresh pasta gives lasagne a creamier consistency," says Onelia. She cooks each sheet individually in bubbling salted water to make this classic Italian dish, which features a flavoursome Bolognese sauce plus milky, buttery béchamel. "The sheets shouldn't break – a minute is enough." Then she leaves the pasta to stand for about 15 minutes on tea towels. "When you can just about see their patterns through the glossy sheets, they're perfect: not too thick and not too thin."

Onelia works at Paul. The company has been sewing jeans for Closed for over 40 years. It is based in Ostra, a small town about 50 kilometres north-west of Ancona. "I've worked there for my whole life," she says. "I started in 1979." Back then, the manufacturer was called Dalmazio after the founder, Dalmazio Galassi. In the 1980s, he handed the firm over to his son Paolo and his brother-in-law Mario, who still own it today. Now, Onelia is responsible for everything that happens before a pair of jeans goes into serial production. "The first samples, to make sure that everything will fit well in the end." It requires a lot of attention to detail.

Onelia has perfected her lasagne over the years. "You shouldn't use a simple cooking wine for the Bolognese sauce. Use a wine you would like to drink with your meal," she says. She recommends a Lacrima di Morro d'Alba. This grape variety is mainly found in the Ancona region and is known for its delicate aroma of cherries and violets.

Onelia creates four or five layers of pasta and sauce, always starting with the pasta, then adding a thin layer of Bolognese sauce followed by a few dollops of béchamel. "Don't do more layers than that. Otherwise the lasagne will be too compact." If any of the lasagne sheets overlap the edges of the dish because they're too big, she carefully folds them over instead of cutting them. Waste not, want not. If it sounds like too much attention to detail, Onelia says: "It's worth the effort because this dish brings everyone together at the dinner table in pure harmony."

And it is true: her lasagne is so fluffy and soft that it puts a smile on the faces of friends, family and colleagues straight away.

Alessandra and Carla's risotto with asparagus

Prep 15 min Cook 45 min Serves 4

500 g white asparagus, peeled and cut into 3–4 cm pieces

2 tbsp olive oil

1 onion, finely chopped

350 g carnaroli rice

50 ml dry white wine

70 g butter

50 g Grana Padano cheese, grated

Salt, pepper

A few basil leaves

There are countless risotto recipes and ways of preparing this creamy dish, which is based on round-grain rice, broth and cheese. For an asparagus risotto, asparagus is first cooked in salted water which is then used instead of stock for the risotto. "The asparagus tips are perfect for garnishing the plate," says Carla.

Alessandra and Carla's risotto with asparagus

The whole family often sits together in Carla's kitchen. And the Holy Christ is always there, too.

CANDY
ARISTON

Boil the asparagus in salted water until al dente. When draining, collect 800 ml of the cooking liquid. Rinse the asparagus with ice water.

Heat the oil in a saucepan. Sauté the onions until colourless. Add the rice and sauté until translucent. Deglaze with wine and boil down briefly. Add enough hot cooking liquid to just cover the rice. Cook uncovered over medium heat for about 15 minutes, stirring with a wooden spoon. Pour in the rest of the hot cooking liquid from time to time.

When the rice is firm to the bite and the risotto is creamy, stir cheese, butter and asparagus pieces, except for the tips, into the risotto. Season with salt and pepper to taste. Decorate with asparagus tips and serve with some basil.

Stir, stir, stir! This makes the risotto creamy – and it prevents it from burning.

Alessandro's ribollita

Prep 20 min Cook 4–5 h Serves 4

1 onion, finely chopped

1 leek, cut into 2–3 cm pieces

2 tbsp olive oil + a little more for drizzling

2 carrots, cut into 2–3 cm pieces

2 small potatoes, cut into 2–3 cm pieces

Salt, pepper

6 stems thyme, leaves plucked off

300 g stale bread, cut into slices

2 tomatoes, diced

100 g green beans, cleaned and cut in half crosswise

2 tins of white beans (drained weight 240 g each)

1 bunch cavolo nero (alternatively tender kale leaves), cut into 4–5 cm wide strips

100 g frozen peas, defrosted

Nowadays, ribollita is mainly prepared using fresh cavolo nero, beans and bread. In days gone by, it was based on the previous day's leftover soup. When it was reheated, its consistency often became so thick that you could use the mixture to make little patties. Ribollita means something like "the warmed up one". "In our family, the recipe has been passed down for generations," says Alessandro.

Sauté the onions and leeks in olive oil in a large pot. Add the potatoes and carrots and fry for about 5 minutes. Salt and pepper to taste. Add the thyme.

Place bread slices on top of the vegetables in the pot. Add 1.5 l hot water and tomatoes and simmer for 30 minutes at medium temperature.

Then simmer gently at a lower temperature for 4–5 hours.

Add beans and cavolo nero 10 minutes before the end of the cooking time.

At the end of the cooking time, add the peas, season with salt and pepper. Finish with a drizzle of olive oil before serving.

“The weekend is for dishes that take a long time to cook.”

Alessandro is responsible for sales and product research at the yarn manufacturer Pecci Filati. The tasks require a lot of time, just like his ribollita. “The longer the soup is cooked, the more intense its aroma becomes.”

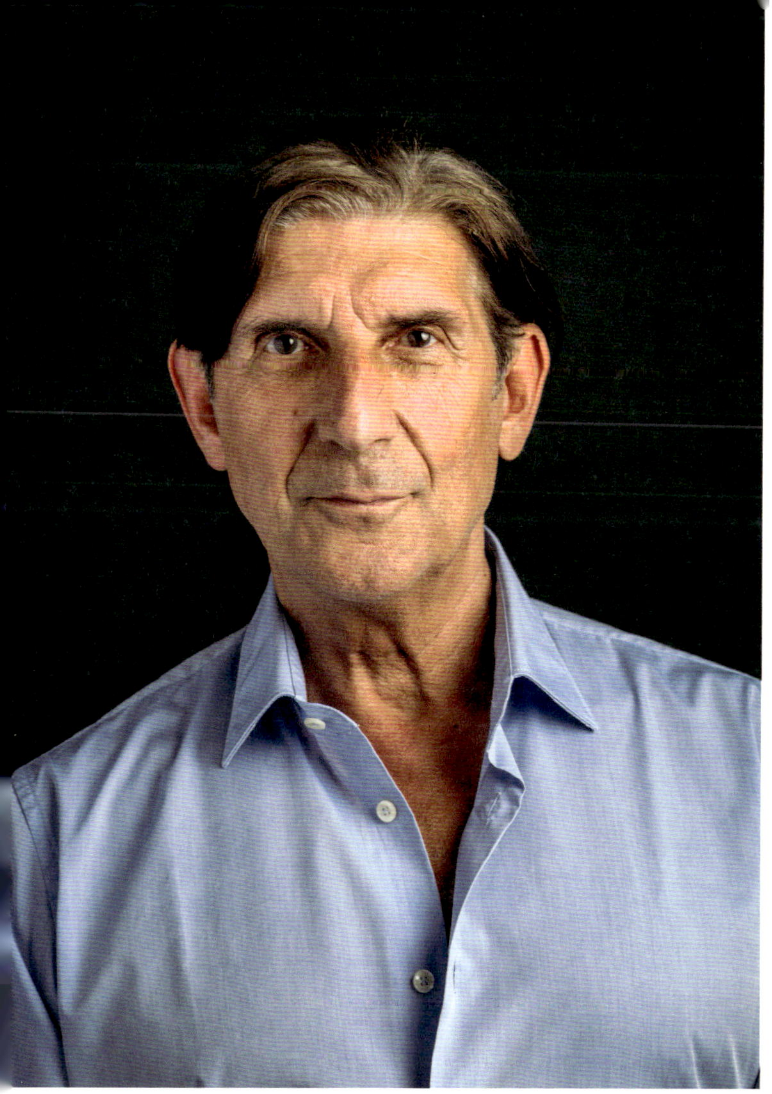

Cavolo nero, beans, kale, carrots, potatoes, onions, tomatoes, leeks and peas – Alessandro's ribollita is packed with vegetables. However, the entire contents of a vegetable patch alone don't make this thick, porridge-like soup so special. The most important ingredient is bread. "It binds a ribollita – and brings all the flavours together," he says. "But it takes time."

Once the vegetables have been chopped and cooked, Alessandro takes a large pot and lines the base with thick slices of bread. Next, he spreads the vegetables on top using a soup ladle and simmers the mixture over a low heat for four to five hours. During this time, the bread soaks up all the liquid and becomes so soft that it disintegrates when the mixture is stirred. In the process, it develops a consistency and flavour that Alessandro describes as "enveloping". "Ribollita makes an ideal weekend meal in autumn or winter," he says.

Alessandro works at Pecci Filati in the village of Campi Bisenzio, which is halfway between Prato and Florence. The world-renowned company produces yarns which are used to make clothing, including high-quality wool and cotton yarns for Closed.

Alessandro joined Pecci Filati in 2001. He works in both sales and product research. This means he is not only interacting with customers and business partners, but also searching for the best materials and ways to improve designs. Just like ribollita, this can also take quite some time.

Alessandro has eaten ribollita since he was a child. "My grandmother always used to make it," he says. Now, he's the one who cooks it. Then and now, ribollita is served with a Brunello di Montalcino. This red wine has a wide range of fruit flavours and contrasts perfectly with the earthy, cabbagey aroma of the soup.

Claudia's cappelletti and ravioli

Prep 1 h   Cook 10 min   Serves 4

For the pasta dough:

4 eggs

300 g wheat flour

100 g durum wheat semolina flour (or more wheat flour)

1 tbsp olive oil

For the ricotta and spinach filling (ravioli):

250 g spinach (fresh or frozen)

200 g ricotta

40 g Parmesan cheese, grated

Nutmeg, grated

Salt, pepper

For the chicken salsiccia filling (cappelletti):

½ chicken breast (approx. 200 g), cut into small pieces

1 salsiccia sausage (approx. 150 g), pressed out of the skin

40 g Parmesan cheese, grated

1 egg, beaten

These small pasta parcels, which resemble tortellini, were first documented in the year 1200. They are traditionally made at Christmas and served in chicken broth. Today, cappelletti and ravioli are also eaten as a classic pasta dish. "They taste heavenly with a tomato or cream sauce," says Claudia.

For the pasta dough, mix eggs, flour and olive oil thoroughly and knead into a smooth dough. Leave to rest in the fridge for 20–30 minutes, wrapped in plastic wrap. Either roll out thinly (approx. 1 mm) or pull into long strips with a pasta machine.

For the ricotta and spinach filling, dry-fry the spinach in a pan and leave to cool slightly. When the spinach is lukewarm, add the other ingredients one by one and mix everything well. Season with salt and pepper to taste.

Cut the rolled-out pasta dough into approx. 4 × 4 cm squares and spread the ricotta and spinach filling on them in small amounts. Fold each square in half to form a triangle and squeeze it shut. If the pasta dough dries out, lightly moisten the edges with a little lukewarm water. Place in boiling water for about 3 minutes. Serve with a sauce of your choice.

For the chicken salsiccia filling, brown the chicken breast pieces and salsiccia meat in a pan. Mince the cooked meat. Make sure that the mixture is not too fine, but still has some structure. Leave to cool. Add the Parmesan and egg and mix well to make a homogeneous paste. Season with salt and pepper to taste.

Cut the rolled-out pasta dough into approx. 4 × 4 cm squares and spread the meat filling on them in small amounts. Fold each square in half to form a triangle. If the pasta dough dries out, lightly moisten the edges with lukewarm water. Bring the corners of the triangle base together, overlap slightly and press together, creating a hat shape (cappelletto means "little hat").

Place in boiling water for about 3 minutes. Traditionally, cappelletti are served with chicken broth as a soup. A meat-free sauce works just as well.

Note: The ravioli and cappelletti can be frozen in freezer bags.

Well equipped: In addition to the rolling pin, a special dough cutter is used.

Claudia's cappelletti and ravioli

Maria fills countless small squares of pasta dough and then artfully folds them shut.

"Cooking and having a glass of white wine: life can be so simple and so good."

Claudia acts as an interface between customers and the in-house design and production team at the denim sewing company Incom. She got her understanding of fashion from her mother Maria – and passed it on to her daughter Shanti. The women live under one roof. "Our favourite thing is to cook together."

In Claudia's home, cooking is a family affair. And when it comes to her cappelletti or ravioli, time is of the essence. Speed is required to make the perfect stuffed pasta parcels because otherwise the pasta dough dries out. "This is definitely a dish that you should only cook with your friends or family," she says.

Claudia lives with her daughter, Shanti, and her mother, Maria, in a house near Pergola, a small village in Marche. Claudia and Maria each have their own quarters which are merged inside the house but have separate outside access. Shanti is there whenever she can get away from her university course in Bologna. They are very much a well-rehearsed team – including when they make cappelletti or ravioli.

Maria has always been in charge of making the pasta dough. It isn't made on an ordinary spianatoia, the board traditionally used in Italy to make pasta and pastry dough, but on a folding pasta table. This is crafted from heavy wood and has a mechanism like a sewing machine table: it unfolds to provide a large work surface for mixing, kneading and rolling; it folds back to hold the rolling pin, the flour whisk and dough scraper, and sits in the kitchen like an ordinary piece of furniture. "In the past, every family in the region had a like this," says Claudia. She and Shanti are expertly cutting small squares from the strips of dough, while Maria oversees rolling out the next strips. A small dollop of the meat mixture is placed on each square and skilfully folded with a few fluid movements.

Working hand in hand with others is also a crucial skill in Claudia's professional life. For the past 16 years she has worked at Incom in the municipality Urbania, where Closed jeans and denim jackets are sewn. "We get the denim from Elena at Candiani (p. 130), and the finished items are then washed by Alberto at Everest (p. 118) or Carlo at Green Lab (p. 32)."

As product coordinator, Claudia is the interface between the in-house design and production team and the fashion brands that order their collection pieces from the company. "First, the customer comes to me with their new designs, explains the fabrics and styles and then I work with our team to see how to implement their wishes." She returns to the customer with the team's feedback. This process is repeated, until everyone agrees and the designs are ordered and produced.

Claudia originally completed a commercial apprenticeship in the textile sector in Switzerland and then went on to study international relations. She turned down an offer from the UN in order to study for a degree in political science in France. Then she became pregnant. "I was 34 and asked myself: do I want a career or do I want to be a mum? Being a mum, I decided, was the better option."

That decision took Claudia back to the Italian countryside and to her parents. They renovated the house. "I did a lot of the work myself – and dug in the soil to make a vegetable garden," she says. "I fell in love with the tranquillity here, and it did me good. There's nothing better than being able to eat your own tomatoes and courgettes." The only thing that was difficult was finding a job that matched her qualifications. "So I thought: fashion! My love of travel, language skills and passion for communication would help to get me a foothold in the sector. And that's exactly what happened."

From an early age, Claudia's daughter Shanti absorbed all these essential skills. Today, she's studying what her mother studied: international relations. Claudia is proud of her daughter's choices. "I think that's great! But what is really interesting is that she devotes all her spare time to fashion. I may know all the brands, but Shanti also knows the designers, stylists and magazines. In our family, everything is interconnected," says Claudia. Fashion, after all, is something of a family tradition, too: "My mother was a seamstress."

What Claudia loves more than anything else is sitting around a table in the garden outside the house with her mother and daughter. "We eat a small dish we prepared ourselves, enjoy a glass of white wine. Life can be so simple and so good."

Plant, sow, harvest: Claudia uses her garden to grow her own vegetables.

Carlo's linguine with ragù

Prep 20 min Cook 1.5 h Serves 4

4 tbsp olive oil

600 g beef braising steak, cut into cubes

Salt, pepper

200 g pancetta, cut into fine strips

2 garlic cloves, finely chopped

200 g celery, finely chopped

200 g carrots, finely chopped

8 tbsp tomato purée

200 ml red wine (dry)

800 g tomatoes (tinned)

1.5 l vegetable stock

320 g linguine

The word ragù has its origins in the French language (ragout means stew). In Italy today, it mainly means a slow-cooked meat sauce with pasta. The classic par excellence is ragù alla Napoletana, which is made from whole pieces of beef and tomatoes. "I like to add bacon to it," says Carlo.

Heat the olive oil in a large pot, add the meat and brown. Season with salt and pepper to taste.

Add the pancetta, garlic, celery and carrots. Stir in the tomato purée. Sauté for approx. 2 minutes at medium heat, then deglaze with red wine and allow to reduce completely. Season with salt and pepper to taste. Add the tomatoes and vegetable stock and simmer over medium heat for approx. 1.5 hours until the meat is very tender and falls apart easily.

Boil the linguine in salted water until al dente and serve with the finished ragù.

Carlo's linguine with ragù

Sara's bigoli with anchovies

Prep 5 min   Cook 15 min   Serves 4

3 tbsp olive oil

1 large white onion, thinly sliced

50 ml dry white wine

10 anchovies, finely chopped

Salt, pepper

400 g bigoli

3–4 stalks parsley, finely chopped

Bigoli was invented in the 15th century at the time of the Venetian–Turkish wars. In 1604, the pasta maker Bartolomeo Veronese had a copper press for making bigoli patented. In Venice, bigoli is traditionally eaten with a sauce made of anchovies, while it is typically served with duck ragù in the Vicenza area. "Because the surface of the pasta is slightly roughened, the sauce sticks well," says Sara.

Put the olive oil in a large frying pan and heat over medium heat. Add the onion slices and sweat them without browning them too much. Deglaze with white wine and 100 ml of water.

Once the onions are translucent, add the anchovies and stir until they are completely dissolved.

Season with salt and pepper to taste.

Cook the bigoli in salted water until al dente. Drain and add to the pan with the sauce.

Stir well. Sprinkle with parsley and serve.

Sara's bigoli with anchovies

"Good food, good clothes: both make you strong and happy."

Sara is responsible for liaising with customers at the button company Cobrax. After work, she likes to treat herself to a plate of pasta. "I like to cook bigoli with anchovies because the dish only needs a few ingredients but it's intensely flavoured."

The advantage of bigoli is obvious to Sara: "It has a rougher surface than other types of pasta," she explains. "That means it holds the sauce better." The strands of pasta are about 25 to 30 centimetres long with a diameter of approximately 2.5 to 3.5 millimetres. This makes them much more substantial than classic spaghetti or linguine. "Sono buoni!"

Sara is a member of the sales team at Cobrax in Padua. Part of the Riri Group, the company makes perfect zips, studs and buttons and specialises in metal buttons which Closed uses for garments such as jeans. Sara focuses on the German market. She liaises with companies there to discuss exactly what they need for their collections and how that can be achieved. "We sell about a million different types of buttons," she says. Sara joined the firm in 2004, initially as an assistant to the owner at the time. "Then I kept progressing through the company." Sara grew up nearby and has eaten bigoli, which originates from the Veneto region, since she was a small child. Bigoli in salsa is served with a salty, creamy sauce made from anchovies and onion. Many families cook this dish on the Friday before a church festival. "People don't eat meat on those days for religious reasons. We always ate bigoli with anchovies at Easter."

There are two secrets behind a portion of really good bigoli in salsa. Firstly, the onions should be sliced wafer-thin so that they develop the right consistency and sweetness when they are lightly fried and braised in white wine. Secondly, after the onions have been mixed with the anchovies, it's important to add one or two ladles of water from the pan to the sauce before it is stirred into the pasta. "That improves the consistency and allows the bigoli to absorb even more flavour."

Alberto's tortellini in broth

Prep 20 min Cook 1.5 h Serves 4

2 onions with skin, halved

2 tbsp oil

1 bunch of soup veg, finely chopped

3–4 sprigs thyme, leaves plucked off and finely chopped

4 cloves

2 bay leaves

1 tbsp black peppercorns

1 boiling chicken, ready to cook (approx. 1.5 kg)

Salt, pepper

1 pinch of sugar

200 g small tortellini (ready-made)

1 small bunch of chives, cut into small rolls

Some Parmesan cheese, grated

Tortellini in broth originally comes from the region of Emilia-Romagna. The pasta parcels are smaller than conventional tortellini. In many Italian families, they are served at Christmas. "The broth is heart-warming" says Alberto.

Roast two onion halves, cut side down, in a large pot for about 3 minutes. Pour in the oil and sauté the veg. Add the other onion, herbs and spices. Put the chicken on the vegetables and pour in about 3 l of cold water.

Salt, bring to the boil and simmer at low heat for about 1.5 hours. Carefully remove the chicken from the broth and leave to cool. It can be used as desired for other dishes (e. g. as a salad topping or wrap filling).

Pour the broth through a sieve into a second pot. Season with salt and pepper to taste, add a pinch of sugar.

Let tortellini steep in the hot chicken broth for 3–4 minutes.

Divide the tortellini and broth between bowls. Serve sprinkled with chives and Parmesan.

Alberto's tortellini in broth

"You can't make good decisions on an empty stomach."

Alberto runs the denim laundry Everest together with his brother. "I need a lot of energy for this job," he says. Nourishing food is therefore a must. Tortellini in broth is his favourite. "Parmesan cheese melted in the broth makes it a real treat."

"I wish I could eat it every day," says Alberto. Tortellini in broth is his favourite food. "You only really eat it in winter though." These little pasta parcels in hot broth are an Italian superfood – nutritious and energising. Alberto needs plenty of energy for his job.

He is one of two managers at Everest, a denim laundry which washes and finishes jeans for Closed. It is located on the outskirts of a small town called Piombino Dese, about 40 kilometres north-west of Venice. Alberto manages the company with his older brother Luca; their father established the firm in 1976. "It started out as a classic laundry with the kind of washing machines you have at home," he says.

Now, it has a production area in excess of 9,000 square metres. This growth is thanks to an early decision to specialise in denim washes. In the 1980s, used denim became trendy for the first time. "Back then, the raw jeans were washed with stones to give them a distressed look," he explains. Now, all sorts of different processes are used. At Everest, for example, there are washes which use lasers or eco-blasters, while creases are added by hand using sandpaper and seams are roughened by carefully running sandpaper over them.

"We always aim to be as eco-friendly as possible, so we don't use any chemicals and we use little or no water." Alberto has also installed a water treatment facility on the roof of his company for environmental reasons. Every day, it purifies approximately 1,200 cubic metres of water. "Innovative technologies, same old quality," he says. It's a good ethos for the future, but it's also important not to forget the past: the original little laundry still exists in the middle of the modern production site.

Although Alberto was born into the company, it was not always clear that he would follow in his father's footsteps. His first passion was football. "I was really good. I might even have been able to play professionally." In the end though, his family was more important. He and his brother joined the company in 2002. "Four years later, my father took a step back. We've been taking care of everything – big and small – ever since." Including tortellini in broth.

Alberto swears by homemade chicken broth. "You just put water, vegetables and a chicken carcass in a pan, then bring it to the boil. Leave it to simmer for an hour and a half," he says. "There's nothing to worry about – it's easy." All that remains is to transfer the broth to a second pan and boil a handful of tortellini in it. Traditionally, the pasta parcels are filled with pork loin, mortadella, Parma ham and Parmesan. "But you can choose whatever you like best," says Alberto. "Just make sure you grate fresh Parmesan on top at the end. When it melts into the broth, it's absolutely delicious."

Barbara's crespelle alla fiorentina

Prep 2.5 h Cook 30 min Serves 4–6

For the filling:

500 g fresh spinach

1 garlic clove, finely chopped

2 tbsp olive oil

400 g fresh ricotta

30 g Pecorino or Parmesan cheese, grated

1 egg

Salt, pepper

Nutmeg, grated

For the crêpes:

3 eggs

250 g wheat flour

500 ml milk

30 g butter

For the béchamel sauce:

100 g butter

100 g flour

1 l fresh whole milk

Nutmeg, grated

For the tomato sauce:

2 tbsp olive oil

1 garlic clove, in its skin

200 g strained tomatoes

A few basil leaves, torn

For gratinating:

A little butter

70 g Pecorino or Parmesan cheese, grated

This crêpe dish became famous in the 16th century, when Caterina Maria Romula di Lorenzo de' Medici became Queen of France. As she didn't enjoy French food, she summoned Italian chefs to the court to prepare her favourite dishes, including crespelle alla fiorentina. "A dish that I love to make for my family," says Barbara.

For the filling, sauté the spinach briefly with the garlic in the olive oil without adding water. Leave to cool, squeeze out the moisture and chop finely. Place in a bowl and mix with ricotta, Pecorino and egg. Salt and pepper to taste, then season with a pinch of nutmeg. Leave to rest in the fridge for an hour.

For the crêpes, crack the eggs into a bowl and whisk with a fork. Sift in the flour and mix to a firm batter without lumps. Gradually add milk and mix well with a whisk until a smooth batter is formed. Add salt and pepper to taste. Cover the bowl with plastic wrap and leave in the fridge for an hour.

Remove the batter from the fridge. Heat a non-stick pan over medium heat. When the pan is hot, lightly grease with butter. Pour about 30 ml of batter into the pan and move the pan around so that the batter is evenly distributed. As soon as the edges of the first crêpe come away from the bottom of the pan, turn it over and place it on a plate. Continue until the batter is used up.

For the béchamel sauce, melt the butter in a pan. Add the flour and sauté for one minute over a very low heat. Pour in the milk, stirring carefully, taking care not to let it boil too much. Once it's boiling, cook for a further 10 minutes, stirring constantly to allow the sauce to thicken. Season with salt and pepper to taste, add a pinch of nutmeg.

For the tomato sauce, heat 2 tbsp olive oil in a pan. Add the garlic and sauté for a few minutes. Add the tomatoes and basil and cook for 15–20 minutes until the sauce thickens a little. Season with salt and pepper to taste.

Preheat the oven to 180 °C. Fill the crêpes with the ricotta and spinach mix. Either roll up the crêpes or fold them into a triangle.

Spread a few tablespoons of béchamel sauce and butter on the bottom of a baking dish and put the crêpes on top. Spread the rest of the béchamel sauce on top, then the tomato sauce and finally the grated cheese. Bake the crêpes for 15–20 minutes until golden brown.

Barbara likes to roll her crespelle. Alternatively, you can fold them like a handkerchief.

Barbara's crespelle alla fiorentina

"Eating is relaxation. The moment when you can forget everything else."

Barbara works in sales at the knitwear manufacturer Pooltrend and focuses on German-speaking countries. When she is not on the road, she enjoys cooking for her loved ones. "I like to show them how important they are to me," she says.

"I grew up with them," says Barbara, of crespelle alla fiorentina – filled, oven-baked crêpes that are typically eaten as a Sunday starter in Florence and the surrounding area. "Now, I don't make them for my family every Sunday because I don't have time, but I always make them for Christmas, Easter and birthdays." A lot of work goes into this dish. That means it is a great way to show people just how much you love them.

First, the filling has to be prepared. "I use ricotta and spinach," says Barbara. To make the filling, the spinach has to be washed and sautéed. Then it is left to cool slightly, the excess water is squeezed out and the leaves are cut into small pieces. Next, it is mixed with cheese, garlic, salt, a little nutmeg and egg. "And after that, the filling has to go in the fridge for an hour to harden and allow the flavour to develop." Next, the batter for the crêpes is made using milk, flour, eggs, salt and butter. "That has to rest in the fridge for an hour, too."

Barbara lives and works in the province of Prato. When she left school, she started working for a yarn manufacturer. In 2014, she joined Pooltrend. Based in the small town of Montemurlo, the company makes knitted accessories for famous fashion brands. Closed has its scarves and blankets made there, for example. "I work in sales and specialise in the German-speaking area," says Barbara. She learnt the language at school and during that time once went on an exchange to Göttingen. "I've loved the country ever since. When I visit partners with my boss, he always says that I start smiling as soon as we cross the Brenner Pass."

When the batter has had an hour in the fridge, Barbara cooks the crêpes one after another in a non-stick pan. "I always use about 30 ml of batter and spread it over the base of the pan. As soon as the edges start curling upwards, I turn the crêpe over." She repeats this time and again until she has a stack of crêpes. Then she makes the béchamel and tomato sauce. Lastly, she fills the crêpes. "Just spread a bit of the ricotta and spinach mixture over the crêpe with a spoon, then roll it up." Afterwards, she puts the rolled-up crêpes in an oven dish, pours the sauces over the top, and bakes them in the oven.

The finished result has a slightly crispy crust and a soft centre. The combination of ricotta, spinach and tomato sauce makes it creamy, fresh and fruity. "You can also fold crespelle alla fiorentina like a handkerchief," adds Barbara. "But I prefer to roll them. That also makes it easy to pick them up and eat them with your fingers when they're cold."

Barbara's crespelle alla fiorentina

Elena's linguine with shrimps

Prep 20 min Cook 15 min Serves 2

200 g datterini tomatoes, halved

2 tbsp olive oil

1 garlic clove in its skin

Salt, pepper

200 g shrimps, ready to cook

50 ml white wine

160 g linguine

Some parsley, finely chopped

150 g stracciatella (or burrata)

Pasta with a quick tomato sauce is part of the basic Italian cuisine. It tastes excellent on its own, but can also be refined with any number of add-ons. Shrimp and stracciatella are popular choices. "The dish is a particularly good choice in spring and summer," says Elena.

Elena's linguine with shrimps

Place the tomatoes in a large, cold pan and slowly reduce them over a low heat. Add the oil and garlic clove. Season with salt and pepper to taste. Simmer for 7–8 minutes. Transfer the tomatoes from the pan to a bowl.

In the same pan, fry the prawns for 2 minutes on each side. Deglaze with white wine. Add the cherry tomatoes.

Boil the linguine in salted water until al dente. Add the linguine to the pan and mix everything together.

Add a little olive oil, pepper and parsley. Arrange on plates and lay stracciatella on top.

Elena's rule of thumb in the kitchen: the fewer ingredients a dish requires, the better their quality should be.

“My basic ingredient when cooking and working: love, lots and lots of love!”

Elena works in the sales team of the denim weaving company Candiani. For her, the company is a special kind of family business: she met her husband at work. After a long day, the two of them like to cook linguine with shrimps. “They taste so good that we forget all about work.”

It starts with the tomatoes, which first have to be reduced. "I halve them and place them in a cold frying pan with the cut side facing down. Only then do I switch the hob on," says Elena. "That lets their juice escape gradually." Her linguine with cherry tomatoes, shrimps and stracciatella cheese – the delicious filling inside a burrata – is a dish that needs to be prepared with care. "Everything has to be cooked on a low heat so that the flavour remains balanced."

For the same reason, when the clove of garlic is added to the pan with the tomatoes, it is left unpeeled. "This stops the flavour from becoming too intense and also prevents it from burning. That would make the sauce bitter." Afterwards, Elena adds white wine to the mixture (she uses an Arneis which she also serves with the finished dish), then she puts the lid on and leaves to simmer for a few minutes.

Elena lives in Turbigo, a little municipality which belongs to the Metropolitan City of Milan. One of the biggest employers in this area is the weaving company Candiani, which produces denim for Closed. Elena is a member of the sales team, so she makes sure communication runs smoothly and deals with partners and companies. "I started here in 2004 after I left university, but I've known the Candiani family since I was little. It's all about family at the company. I even met my husband there," she says. Strictly speaking, she was introduced to him there before they even met. When she was 14, her father – who also worked at Candiani – took her with him to work one day. "He introduced me to his colleagues, including a man who said he had the perfect boyfriend for me at home – his son. Ten years later, I met him at work and married him," she says. Now, she and her husband have a son. "I often cook linguine for them. It's a special dish, but it doesn't take long to make."

As soon as the tomato sauce thickens, Elena pours it into a pasta bowl and cooks the shrimps on a low heat in the pan. She puts the pasta in a saucepan and returns the tomatoes to the frying pan when the shrimps are cooked. Lastly, she adds the pasta and stirs everything together. "To make the linguine look really good on the plate, I suggest using tongs to twist it into a nest shape inside a ladle, then carefully putting it down. That keeps it together. Then garnish it with a few shrimps and scatter stracciatella and a little finely chopped parsley over the top."

Amore per sempre:
Pasta and tomatoes
simply belong together!

PEÑA FRESH

Paola's gnocchi with tomatoes and cinnamon

Prep 40 min   Cook 30 min   Serves 4

For the gnocchi:

1 kg potatoes

300 g flour + a little more for the work surface

1 egg + 1 egg yolk, beaten

Salt, pepper

For the sauce:

2 tbsp oil

1 onion, finely chopped

1 garlic clove, finely chopped

1.5 kg tomatoes, diced

Some basil leaves, torn

1–2 tbsp cinnamon

Gnocchi means "knots in wood". The little dumplings are traditionally made from semolina (dating back to ancient Rome) or from potato (since the 18th century). There are many variations featuring this type of pasta. "Gnocchi with tomatoes and cinnamon has been cooked in my family for generations at carnival time," says Paola.

Boil the potatoes until they are soft. Peel the potatoes while still hot and mash finely with a potato masher. Leave mashed potatoes to cool on a lightly floured work surface. Add the egg. Season with salt and pepper to taste. Gradually knead the flour into the potato mixture.

Form 2–3 cm thick rolls from the potato dough. Cut into 2 cm pieces and roll over the back of a lemon grater (or press in with the tines of a fork). Place on a floured surface.

For the sauce, put the oil in a pan, fry onion for about 5 minutes, add the garlic. After 2–3 minutes, add the tomatoes and some of the basil. Add salt and pepper to taste. Simmer on a low heat for 30 minutes. Then pour everything through a sieve into a smaller pot. Simmer the sauce for another 30 minutes. Season with salt and pepper to taste, add the cinnamon.

Put the gnocchi into boiling salted water. Cook until they rise to the surface. Serve with sauce and some basil.

Paola's gnocchi with tomatoes and cinnamon

Paola rolls her gnocchi over the back of a lemon grater. This adds texture, and they hold more sauce later.

"Fashion and food have to look good. Taste begins with appearance."

At shoe specialist Stil Tre, Paola makes sure that nothing goes wrong with the production of a new collection, from manufacturing to delivery. "Shoemaking has been with me since I was a child," she says. "So has the way I shape gnocchi."

Paola uses a clever trick to make sure her gnocchi can hold lots of sauce. Ever so carefully, with the palm of her hand, she rolls the dumplings over the back of a lemon grater. Doing this gives the gnocchi a pattern of ridges, making them look a bit like pine cones. This means that the sweet tomato and cinnamon sauce really clings to them once they have been cooked. "It takes a bit of practice to get gnocchi al pomodoro e cannella right, but it's worth it," she says.

Paola learnt how to roll gnocchi over many years. As a little girl, she used to watch her mother preparing them. Then, one day, she was allowed to have a go, too. "We always ate this dish on Venerdì Gnocolar." In and around Verona, this is the name given to the last Friday in the carnival season. Every family cooks their favourite gnocchi recipe on that day. This tradition stems from the Middle Ages, when many people in the city were starving. "The wealthy people decided to give them basic foodstuffs like gnocchi," says Paola. Because they did this on the last Friday in the carnival season, it is still traditional to eat gnocchi on that day.

Paola works at Stil Tre. Located in an idyllic place called San Giovanni Ilarione east of Verona, this producer makes footwear for Closed. There are a lot of shoemakers in this area, so that is something else that Paola grew up with. "I started making shoes as soon as I left school," she says. Now, she makes sure that manufacturing runs smoothly at Stil Tre, all the way from when a new collection goes into production to when it is delivered.

Everyone should try her trick for getting more sauce on gnocchi. As well as enhancing this tomato and cinnamon dish, it makes lots of other sauces – salsa, pesto, sugo and ragù – taste even better. "Gnocchi used to be something that poor people ate, so it makes sense not to waste any sauce."

Carlo's cannelloni with ricotta cheese and artichokes

Prep 1.5 h* Cook 30 min Serves 8

For the pasta dough:

500 g wheat flour

5 eggs

* Alternatively: ready-made cannelloni (shortens the prep time by around 45 min)

For the filling:

400 g ricotta

300 g Parmesan cheese, grated

Zest of two organic lemons

For the topping:

6 artichokes

3 tbsp olive oil

2 garlic cloves, finely chopped

Salt, pepper

For the béchamel sauce:

80 g butter

100 g wheat flour

800 ml milk

These pasta tubes are traditionally filled with a rich, meaty sauce. The dish was invented in Naples in the early 20th century. There are now dozens of different ways of filling cannelloni. "My vegetarian alternative is made with creamy ricotta, lemons and slightly bitter artichokes. It tastes like summer," says Carlo.

Carlo's cannelloni with ricotta cheese and artichokes

For the pasta dough, mix 500 g flour and the eggs. Spread the flour on the work surface, add the eggs and knead for about 20 minutes until you have a smooth pasta dough. Leave to rest in plastic wrap in the fridge.

For the topping, remove the stems and hard outer leaves from the artichokes. Cut off the top part of the artichokes and remember to remove the chokes.

Cut the remaining parts of the artichokes into 2–3 cm pieces and put them in a pan with the olive oil and garlic. Salt and pepper to taste. Fry the artichokes over medium heat until they are soft.

For the filling, mix the ricotta with 100 g Parmesan and the lemon zest. Season with salt and pepper to taste. If the mixture is very firm, add a drop of milk.

Roll out the pasta dough very thinly (approx. 2 mm) with a pasta machine or a rolling pin. Cut approx. 10 × 10 cm squares from the dough. Boil them in salted water for 20 seconds, rinse in cold water and hang on strings to dry or pat dry with paper towels.

For the béchamel sauce, melt the butter in a pan. Add 100 g flour and sauté for one minute over very low heat. Pour in the milk, stirring carefully, taking care not to let it boil too much. Once it's boiling, cook for a further 10 minutes, stirring constantly to allow the sauce to thicken. Season with salt and pepper to taste.

To make the cannelloni, fill the pasta squares evenly with the ricotta filling and roll them up. Alternatively, fill ready-made cannelloni using a piping bag with a nozzle.

Preheat the oven to 160 °C. Spread 2 tbsp béchamel sauce on the bottom of a baking dish. Place the stuffed cannelloni in the dish and arrange the artichokes on top.

Spread the béchamel sauce evenly over the top and sprinkle with the remaining Parmesan. Bake in the preheated oven for approx. 30 minutes until the surface is lightly browned.

No pasta machine? No problem!
The dough can simply be rolled out
with a rolling pin.

AGLIO
FAVE
CARCIOFI
DI
CASA

Azienda Agricola Marchetti

Wine not?

Maurizio's winery is just south of Ancona. His Azienda Agricola Marchetti not only produces the finest Rosso Conero DOC. It is also home to an old family castle.

Some way down the Via di Pontelungo going south from Ancona, off the main road and along a bumpy gravel path, lies an unassuming property at the foot of some rolling hills. The detour to no. 116 is more than worth it: at the end of the track is a small but exquisite vineyard run by a vintner named Maurizio Marchetti. In the dark cellar beneath his house, wines mature to perfection. In the tasting room next to it, a table and a couple of chairs are surrounded by old wine barrels that function as a bar. Maurizio isn't a man to make a big fuss about the presentation of his wine; he prefers to focus on the product. Helped by a handful of employees, every year he produces around 50,000 bottles of wines which are typical of the region.

The Marche nestles between the Apennines and the Adriatic Sea. The west is characterised by limestone soil, while in the east the vineyards extend all the way to the coast and the foot of Mount Conero, which lends its name to Rosso Conero DOC. This controlled designation of origin was introduced in 1967. According to the rules, this fruity, balanced red wine must consist of at least 85 per cent Montepulciano with the addition of no more than 15 per cent of the other grape varieties permitted for cultivation in the region. As well as this wine, Maurizio produces Verdicchio Classico, the famous straw-yellow, dry white wine of the Marche.

Maurizio is more than happy to tell visitors all about the region and its wines. He enjoys welcoming guests on the small terrace in front of the tasting room, accompanied by his dog Tea. "My son found her in a field, where she had been abandoned. Now she lives a good life with us," he says.

The first vines grow on the inland side of the gravel road. The area is modest – not far from here Marchetti owns a much larger vineyard. Maurizio has 16 hectares for red wine and eight for white wine. Not all the areas are connected, because even though his family has lived here for over five generations, the Azienda Agricola Marchetti vineyard was only founded a generation ago by Maurizio's father, who kept on adding new fields. Maurizio's great-great-grandfather was a spice merchant. In a small pine copse where old stone walls are just visible between the trunks lies what Maurizio calls the "family treasure" – a small castle with interior walls decorated with frescoes of sailors loading ships with cinnamon, caraway and all kinds of other spices. There are seven rooms on the first floor and a ballroom on the ground floor with French windows, a sprung parquet floor and chandeliers. "Nobody wants to live here, it's much too expensive to run," Maurizio explains. The castellino remains a sleeping beauty, visited regularly only by the dog: "Tea loves to play here."

Although Maurizio was born into the vineyard, he studied agricultural science, giving him solid expertise that now benefits the family enterprise. He views wine-making as a combination of mathematics and art, and loves experimenting and finding new solutions. Driven by this inventive spirit, Maurizio is constantly adding new wines to his range. The sparkling wines, which are increasingly popular, are crisp and lovely but no one should leave the winery without a real Rosso Conero. His Castro Di San Silvestro, made with Montepulciano, Sangiovese and Syrah grapes, is a deep ruby red in colour, and harmonises well with braised meats, but also with rich pasta dishes. For the best flavour it should be opened and left to breathe an hour before serving in order to bring out the aromas of dark cherries, a hint of plum and the slightly woody note. "A good wine needs time," adds Maurizio.

The wine-growing areas of the Azienda Agricola Marchetti extend over around 24 hectares.

Montepulciano is one of Maurizio's main grape varieties.

Secondi

The second main course – now we're serving meat and fish!
From baked monkfish to arista pork roast or Venetian-style calves' liver

Fabrizio's
barbecued fish
156

Luana's pork fillet
in puff pastry
164

Stella's peposo
dell'Impruneta
168

Lorenzo's
arista pork roast
174

Veronica's baccalà
182

Antonio's lamb
skewers
186

Alessandra and
Carla's fried chicken
190

Marco's Venetian-
style calves' liver
192

Daniela's
baked monkfish
198

Fabrizio's barbecued fish

Prep 20 min Cook 20 min Serves 2

300 g catch of the day
(e. g. mackerel or sea bream)

100 g dry bread

50 ml olive oil

2 garlic cloves, peeled

Salt, pepper

20 g basil leaves

30 g parsley leaves

The tradition of cooking over an open fire with just a few ingredients is centuries old. In Italy, they call it grigliata – and distinguish between grigliata di pesce (fish), grigliata di carne (meat) and grigliata mista (fish and meat). "Everything tastes better with subtle roasted flavours," says Fabrizio.

Mix bread, olive oil, salt and black pepper in a blender.

When the mixture is ready, blend in the basil and parsley leaves until it becomes bright green. The mixture should not be too fine with some bigger pieces in it. Cover the fish with the bread mix.

Make a hot flame, roast the fish once the coal becomes white.

Fabrizio's barbecued fish

"If you want to work well together, you have to be able to eat well together."

Fabrizio works in sales at the denim laundry Green Lab. He has known the family business since the beginning, and his current boss almost since he was born. After work, the two of them sometimes have a barbecue together. "My favourite is barbecued fish coated with breadcrumbs and parsley!"

For Fabrizio, barbecued fish isn't just barbecued fish. "This dish celebrates the beauty of life." He lives on the coast, south of Ancona, where he grew up. The Mediterranean has always been a well-stocked pantry to him. "Barbecued fish is a reward which you should enjoy with family or friends after a hard day's work."

Fabrizio works at Green Lab, an eco-conscious denim laundry in the village of Grottammare, about 80 kilometres away from Ancona. Closed has its jeans washed and finished there. Fabrizio works in sales, which means he liaises with clients and partners. "Everything crosses my desk, from the first price negotiations to the final delivery. I oversee the whole process to make sure nothing goes wrong," he says.

Green Lab is a third-generation family business. "I've known the company for 33 years and have worked with all three generations. I met my current boss, Carlo (p. 32), when he was just a few days old." This doesn't make it difficult for Fabrizio to work for him though. "Carlo has new ideas that keep me young. Meanwhile, he can rely on all the experience that I've gained over the course of three decades. It couldn't be any better, could it?"

That is precisely why Fabrizio and Carlo often meet up and barbecue fish together. Theoretically, any fish can be barbecued. Fabrizio buys fish from the local market, choosing whatever has been caught that day just a stone's throw away. Today, for example, it's sea bream. There are a few squid, too. "They taste great with subtle roasted flavours as well." Whatever fish is being barbecued, the coating is crucial. It is a mixture of breadcrumbs and fresh parsley known as "pangrattato e prezzemolo". Those who want an extra burst of freshness can stir in a little lemon zest, too. "After gutting and washing the fish, you simply coat it well with the mixture of bread and seasoning, then clip it into a fish basket." This is a hinged wire basket which allows you to barbecue the fish evenly and stops it from falling apart. The barbecue mustn't be too hot, though. "Fish is sensitive. If you want to play it safe, put it at the edge where it's a bit cooler."

Fresh bread and salad are, he believes, the best side dishes to serve with grigliata di pesce. As for drink,"Prosecco is good, or a fruity, mineral white wine like Pecorino, which is typical of our region," says Fabrizio. "Or why not have a glass of each to mark the occasion?"

The coating for the barbecued fish consists of breadcrumbs and fresh parsley. In Italian: "pangrattato e prezzemolo".

Fabrizio's barbecued fish

A view of the sea: south of the town of Senigallia.

Luana's pork fillet in puff pastry

Prep 30 min   Cook 35 min   Serves 4

1 pork fillet (600–800 g)

Salt, pepper

2 tbsp olive oil

100 g pancetta or bacon, thinly sliced

1 sheet of puff pastry, rectangular (refrigerated)

100 g cheese, sliced (e. g. Provolone)

1 egg yolk

The story goes that Arthur Wellesley, 1st Duke of Wellington, asked to be served a fillet of beef in puff pastry after his victory over Napoleon in 1815. Now, all sorts of dishes consisting of meat wrapped in pastry are considered to stem from this dish. "We have pork fillet in puff pastry on special occasions," says Luana.

Season the pork with salt and pepper to taste. Place in a pan with oil and fry on medium to high heat until brown on all sides. Leave to cool for about 30 minutes. Then wrap the pork fillet in the pancetta slices until the entire surface is covered.

Preheat the oven to 180 °C. Roll out the puff pastry (approx. 3 mm) and cover it evenly with cheese slices. Make sure to leave 3–4 cm free at the edge of the puff pastry so that the cheese does not run out during baking.

Wrap the cheesy puff pastry around the pork and pancetta so that the cheese and pancetta meet. Press the puff pastry surface smoothly and seal well. Brush the surface with egg yolk. Bake in the oven at 180 °C for 30–35 min.

Luana's pork fillet in puff pastry

"Creating something means bringing joy to other people."

Luana is a pattern maker at the denim sewing company Incom, so she is responsible for bringing designs of new garments to life. "I like to work with my hands," she says, "even when I'm cooking. Pork fillet wrapped in puff pastry might take some practice, but once you get the hang of it, it's really easy."

"Everyone likes serving a roast or a nice piece of meat on special occasions," says Luana. However, some meat dishes can be tricky to get right every time. "Filetto di maiale in crosta is fail-safe," she says. It consists of a fillet of pork wrapped in puff pastry with a thin layer of melted cheese and crispy bacon in between. The secret to success is to sear each side of the meat first, then leave it to cool for about 30 minutes. "That allows it to start cooking before it is covered with all the other ingredients and put in the oven."

Luana has been working at Incom since 2005. The company sews jeans and denim jackets for Closed and draws on craftsmanship and innovativeness. It is based in the town of Urbania, about a 90-minute drive west of Ancona. Luana is a pattern maker, meaning that she brings designs for new garments to life by transforming sketches into prototypes. "I translate designers' ideas into three-dimensional mock-ups," she explains.

She mainly works on designs for Closed. "The longer I work for a client, the better I understand them. Over the years, you get to know what they want." The thing she likes best about her job is creating something with her own hands. "At the end of the day, I can see what I've done."

Luana likes using her hands to cook, too. She rolls out the puff pastry until it is about three millimetres thick and then arranges slices of cheese on top. "You need to leave some space around the edge so that the cheese doesn't ooze out in the oven," she says. Once the meat has cooled, she wraps it in bacon and then places it in the middle of the layer of cheese. "If the meat was still hot, the cheese would start melting now and everything wouldn't stick together so well."

Luana carefully folds the end of the puff pastry over the meat, then rolls it up from bottom to top. She gently presses down the edges and the open ends. "You can trim any excess pastry," she says. It might take a bit of practice, but anyone who makes this dish should remember that it is not a beauty contest. In the oven, the pastry rises anyway so that any lumps and bumps disappear. "And the meat is so tender and juicy that no one will care about anything except the taste!"

Stella's peposo dell'Impruneta

Prep 10 min Cook 3 h Serves 4

2 tbsp black peppercorns

1 kg beef braising steak (not too lean), cut into 3–4 cm cubes

400 g strained tomatoes (tinned)

8 cloves garlic, peeled

1 small bunch of sage, leaves plucked off and finely chopped + some more for garnishing

1 small bunch of rosemary, leaves plucked and finely chopped

Salt

1 l Chianti (or other dry red wine)

"Da peposo" means "peppered". Impruneta is a small town just outside Florence, where clay tiles for the dome of Santa Maria del Fiore were made in the 15th century. The dish is said to have come from there. "It is important to let it stew for a long time so that the meat is tender," says Stella.

Grind the peppercorns (e.g. in a sealed freezer bag using a rolling pin).

Peposo is traditionally cooked in a clay pot in the oven. Alternatively, to prepare it on the hob, layer meat, tomatoes, garlic, pepper and herbs in a pot. Season with salt to taste.

Pour in red wine until everything is just covered. Cook over medium heat with the lid on for at least 3 hours until the meat is tender. Stir occasionally and check that there is enough liquid. Otherwise add a little more wine. Season to taste with salt.

Preparation in the oven: cook at 160 °C with the lid on for 1.5 hours. Then cook without a lid at 180 °C for a further 1.5 hours until the meat is tender. Check from time to time that there is enough liquid, otherwise add a little wine. Season to taste with salt. Serve with Tuscan bread.

"Made in Italy is an important quality mark for fashion and food."

Stella works in sales for the yarn manufacturer Pecci Filati. In the kitchen, she prefers hearty dishes. She grew up with peposo dell'Impruneta. "As a child, I couldn't wait until they finally took the lid off and let me taste it," she says.

Stella's earliest memory of peposo is its smell. "The way the aroma of the ingredients slowly develops during the hours of stewing," she says. The dish contains beef, lots of black pepper, garlic, sage, rosemary and Chianti. "As a child, I couldn't wait until the lid finally came off and I could try it."

Stella is an export sales manager at Pecci Filati, a yarn manufacturer which supplies Closed with wool and cotton. Her job is to sell new products and collections all around the world. Pecci Filati is located in Campi Bisenzio, which belongs to the Metropolitan City of Florence.

Stella has been working there for over 30 years. She was born in the town of Prato, just a few kilometres away. "I'm Tuscan through and through," she says. "Peposo is a typical Tuscan dish." It uses relatively cheap beef shank, which has to be cooked for a long time to make it really tender. "It's important not to cut it up too small," says Stella. Otherwise, you end up with ragù. Peposo is traditionally stewed in a large clay dish and is often served in matching little bowls. It is mainly eaten in winter. The best wine to complement it is a fruity Chianti. "From controlled cultivation and – of course – from Tuscany!"

This beef stew is said to date back to when Florence Cathedral, with its famous dome by Filippo Brunelleschi, was built. The legend goes that when the ovens used to make roof tiles for the dome were still hot, meat was stewed inside them in clay pots to give the workers a filling meal which would keep them going. "Peposo was something poor people ate," says Stella.

ORECCHIETTE
BARESI
FATTE A MANO
ETTO
PANE di LATERZA
Cotto nel forno a legna
FORNERIE LAERTINE
Euro 4,80 al Kg
CHÂTEAU
PEZ
6 Btles
GRAHAM
VSOP
Maldon
SEA SALT
POMODORI
SECCHI
€10.00
AL KILO
CIPOLLE
di TROPEA
I.G.P
ZZARELLA DI BUFALA CAMPA
OMINAZIONE DI ORIGINE PRO

PORTO FEIST CUVEE 1944
PORTO KROHN COLHEITA 1980
JAMES EADIE
BOLLINGER
LOUIS ROEDERER
NIPOZZANO
MANICARDI
ROUGIÉ
OLIVE CONDITE € 1,60
OLIVE TAGGIASCHE € 2.80
POMODORI € 2.50 ETTO
ALICI € 3.00
POLPO € 4.00 ETTO
SGOMBRO € 3.00
BOTTARGA DI TONNO ROSSO

Lorenzo's arista pork roast

Prep 20 min Cook 1h 10 min Serves 4–6

800 g pork saddle with thin fat cover (boneless)

3 tbsp olive oil

1 tbsp butter

Salt, pepper

200–300 ml white wine

1 clove of garlic, finely chopped

A few sprigs of rosemary, leaves plucked off and finely chopped (optional: more sprigs)

6–8 potatoes, peeled and cut into 3–4 cm pieces

Kitchen string

This dish was given its name in the 15th century. In 1432, ecclesiastical dignitaries met for a feast at the Council of Florence. They described a seasoned pork joint served there as "aristos", in other words: excellent. "And that's exactly how it tastes," says Lorenzo.

Lorenzo cuts up the rosemary and garlic with a mezzaluna knife. Salt and pepper are also added to the seasoning for the roast.

Tie the pork saddle with kitchen string to form a joint. Score the meat lightly with a knife.

Preheat the oven to 180 °C. Heat the oil and butter in a large ovenproof pan. Put the meat in the pan, season it with salt and pepper to taste. Sear well on all sides, turning several times. Remove the meat from the pan. Deglaze the pan with 100 ml wine, let it evaporate briefly over a high heat. Remove the pan from the heat and put the meat back into the pan.

Mix the garlic and rosemary and spread over the meat. Add the potato pieces. Season with salt and pepper to taste. Remove the pan, meat and potatoes from the hob and place in the oven. Cook for 30 minutes, turning occasionally.

Add more wine. Cook for another 40–45 minutes. Occasionally spoon the cooking liquid over the meat to make it more tender.

For even more flavour, Lorenzo adds whole rosemary sprigs in addition to the chopped rosemary.

"With good food, some problems disappear into thin air."

Lorenzo works in the sales department of the knitwear manufacturer Pooltrend. This job is a dream come true for him. "I always wanted to work in fashion," he says. The perfect reward for him after a long day's work is an arista roast pork. "It's my favourite family recipe. My grandmother used to make it."

"When I think of arista, I don't just think of the food itself. I think of the special people and feelings that I associate with it," says Lorenzo. Arista is a juicy piece of pork loin which is roasted with a handful of herbs until it is beautifully tender. This Florentine roast is a typical Sunday meal. "It's a family meal. My grandmother always used to make it for us."

Lorenzo grew up in the province of Prato and attended the Tullio Buzzi textile college. "I always wanted to work in fashion," he says. He started his career in the technical department at a production facility and is now part of the Pooltrend sales team. "It's a dream come true. Managing accounts, having my own clients, liaising with them and offering them products." Pooltrend is located in the small town of Montemurlo and is renowned for its knitted accessories. Closed has products like scarves made there.

It doesn't take long to prepare Lorenzo's arista. "First, you have to chop the garlic and rosemary." Lorenzo puts them on a chopping board, scatters salt and pepper over the top, and chops them into small pieces with a mezzaluna knife. "That instantly creates a great blend of seasoning."

Next, he wraps string around the joint several times to hold it together in the oven and carefully scores it with a knife. He rubs the seasoning into the meat, cuts a few potatoes into small pieces (these make the perfect side) and puts everything in a shallow oven dish. It is then roasted for 80 to 90 minutes. To give the meat even more flavour and tenderness, white wine can be poured over it after about 30 minutes. "To make sure the joint cooks evenly, turn it a few times and baste it regularly using a small ladle or spoon. That makes the meat juicier."

LIMONI al NATURALE
SICILIA
AL KILO
€3.00
di Costiera
089 877593 profumodicostiera@gmail.com

Veronica's baccalà

Prep 15 min   Cook 3 h   Serves 2–4

250 g onions, sliced

250 ml olive oil

2 anchovies, finely chopped

1 bunch parsley, finely chopped

600 g stockfish, cut into 2–3 cm pieces

250 ml milk

100 g flour

30 g Parmesan cheese, grated

Salt, pepper

Baccalà alla vicentina is unusual in that there are records showing exactly when the dish was invented. In 1432, the ship's captain Pietro Querini brought dried cod home with him from a research voyage to the outer islands of Norway. The cooks on Querini's ship were so taken with the product that they used it straight away – as did the people in Veneto, where the ship docked. "The recipe has been passed down in my family for generations," says Veronica.

Put about 100 g of the onions in a saucepan and fry with olive oil. Add the anchovies and parsley and brown for 5 minutes.

Add the stockfish and fry for 5 minutes. Add the remaining onions, milk, flour, Parmesan and 2 tbsp olive oil to the stockfish. Season with salt and pepper to taste.

Simmer for 3 hours in the pot with the lid on over a low heat.

Serve in traditional style with grilled polenta.

"Never work or cook in a hurry – you will get better results."

Veronica takes care of everything that happens before production at the shoe specialist Stil Tre: the individual parts, patterns, laces and soles. She loves to eat baccalà with her family. "It's one of those dishes that makes you happy with the first bite."

"The most important thing is the fish," says Veronica. Luckily, nowadays no one has to soak a baccalà for days before it can be used. The heavily salted, air-dried cod is now available ready to use by the name of "stoccafisso ammollato". This is the key ingredient in Veronica's baccalà alla vicentina, a traditional stew from the Veneto region.

"My mother and grandmother come from there," says Veronica. "The recipe is handed down from generation to generation in my family." It hasn't changed much over the years. Onions, anchovies, milk, Parmesan and parsley are simmered in a pan with the baccalà for several hours to make a rich, creamy stew. "It's one of those dishes that make you happy with the very first bite, so it's perfect comfort food for winter, served with grilled polenta."

Veronica works at Stil Tre. Located in an idyllic place called San Giovanni Ilarione east of Verona, this producer makes footwear for Closed. "I take care of what happens before the shoes are made," she says. "I source all the individual components – soles and shoelaces, leather and other materials – and work out the price of the finished product based on that." Veronica originally studied industrial psychology. Although it might seem to have nothing to do with making shoes, "Each project is ultimately about accommodating different opinions, i. e. teamwork."

Veronica knows that it is important to have the right sparring partners at the dinner table as well as at work, so she recommends a dry white wine with her baccalà. "The fish is salty, so the wine shouldn't be too full flavoured."

Antonio's lamb skewers

Prep 30 min   Cook 20 min   Serves 4

520 g lamb, cut into approx. 1 cm cubes

2 tbsp olive oil

1 clove garlic, finely chopped

1 tsp oregano

1 tsp rosemary

1 tsp chilli powder

Salt, pepper

8 wooden skewers

These barbecued lamb skewers are an Abruzzo speciality. The meat is diced, marinated and cooked on a special charcoal barbecue until it is crispy. This recipe is said to come from shepherds who used to move around with their herds and sleep in the fields. "Food that you prepare for a group of friends," says Antonio.

Soak the wooden skewers in water for 30 minutes before barbecuing.

Mix the lamb with olive oil, garlic and spices. Season with salt and pepper to taste. Leave to marinate for 30 minutes.

Put the lamb cubes on the skewers, alternating lean and fattier pieces.

Heat the barbecue to approx. 260 °C. Barbecue the meat skewers over high direct heat, turning several times, until the meat is cooked and browned on all sides.

Season again with salt and pepper to taste.

Serve the finished lamb skewers with toasted garlic bread and a fresh salad.

Antonio's lamb skewers

Lamb skewers are called arrosticini in Italian. They are traditionally served from a specially designed jar.

Alessandra and Carla's fried chicken

Prep 20 min Cook 15 min Serves 4

2 eggs

Salt, pepper

100 g breadcrumbs

100 g flour

500 g chicken breast,
cut into approx. 3 cm pieces

250 ml oil for frying

The Italian version of fried chicken is called bocconcini di pollo impanati. The coating is only breadcrumbs, which makes it more delicate than its American counterpart. The precursor of this dish is pullum frontonianum, a fried chicken dish first mentioned in a Roman cookbook from the fourth century. "It has to be served hot," says Alessandra.

Beat the eggs in a shallow bowl. Season with salt and pepper.

Put the flour and breadcrumbs in a shallow bowl each. Season with salt and pepper.

To coat, first turn the chicken pieces in the flour until they are evenly coated. Roll lightly between your hands, carefully tapping off any excess flour. Then gradually dip the chicken pieces in the egg and turn them in the breadcrumbs until they are evenly coated on all sides. Carefully place the finished breaded pieces on a plate without overlapping.

Heat the oil. When hot, fry the breaded chicken pieces in it until golden brown. After frying, drain briefly on kitchen paper and serve immediately.

Alternatively, bake the chicken in the oven at 200 °C for 15 minutes. Serve with potatoes.

Alessandra and Carla's fried chicken

Marco's Venetian-style calves' liver

Prep 10 min Cook 15 min Serves 2

60 g butter

2 tbsp olive oil

2 large onions, cut into fine rings

400 g calves' liver,
cut into strips about 2 cm wide

Salt, pepper

2 cl brandy

1 tbsp white wine vinegar

1 sprig rosemary, leaves plucked off
and finely chopped

1 sprig sage, leaves plucked off
and finely chopped

1 bay leaf

Liver is one of the best-known dishes in the history of Roman cuisine. The ancient Romans ate it with figs to offset the strong flavour of the liver with something sweeter. Later on, the Venetian version with onions became popular because they were more readily available all year round. "It is refined with brandy," says Marco.

Heat half the butter in a pan. Add the olive oil. Sauté the onions over medium heat until they are transllucent. Increase the heat. Season the liver with salt and pepper. Add it to the pan and fry well for2–3 minutes.

Deglaze the liver with brandy and vinegar and heat to just below boiling point. Stir in the remaining butter and thicken the sauce with it. Add the herbs and continue cooking for a few minutes. Serve with polenta or bread.

Marco's Venetian-style calves' liver

"When the right product is prepared in the right way, everyone likes it."

Marco takes care of dyeing fabrics at the denim laundry Everest. "It's a physical job, but I like to get things done. That's probably why I also enjoy cooking so much," he says. Venetian-style calves' liver is one of his favourite dishes. "I've loved it since I was a kid."

"A lot of people shy away from liver because it has a strong taste of its own," says Marco. "But everyone should try the right product prepared in the right way. It can be much milder." Fegato alla Veneziana – Venetian-style calves' liver – is his magic formula. Made with lots of fresh herbs and onions, it only takes a few minutes to prepare.

First, the onions are cooked until they are transparent, then removed from the pan. Next, thin strips of liver are fried lightly with rosemary, sage and bay leaves. Brandy and vinegar are added, then the onions are returned to the pan and the mixture is braised for about ten minutes. That's it! "The herbs give the meat a fresh flavour and the brandy adds a sweet finishing touch," says Andrea. He recommends serving it with fresh bread. Even as a child, he enjoyed this dish. "I wouldn't eat the onions though. I didn't like vegetables."

Marco works at Everest, a denim laundry which washes and finishes jeans for Closed. It is located on the outskirts of a small town called Piombino Dese, about 40 kilometres north-west of Venice. Marco is a dyeing specialist. He mixes dyes and oversees the process which gives denim its distinctive appearance in a wide range of blues. "I like working with my hands, which is probably why I also enjoy cooking."

He used to work part-time as a restaurant chef alongside his main job. "One or two days during the week; at the weekend sometimes, too. There came a point where it was too much though." Now, Marco prefers to spend his time with his family. Thanks to his time as a chef, he knows which wines go with which dishes. "With Venetian-style calves' liver, I recommend a red wine which isn't too heavy. Cabernet Sauvignon is perfect, or a Pinot Noir."

Leoni
Leoni
PIAZZA
Melasì
Melasì

Daniela's baked monkfish fillets

Prep 15 min Bake 1 h Serves 4

600–700 g monkfish fillets

3–4 large potatoes, peeled

Salt, pepper

1 onion, finely diced

2 tbsp olive oil

A dash of white wine

A bunch of parsley, finely chopped

1 tbsp thyme leaves, finely chopped

250 g cherry tomatoes, halved

Black olives

This dish is served in Italy all year round, but is increasingly popular at Christmas as an alternative to meat. Daniela learnt how to make it a few years ago by watching a friend. "If you have guests, you can easily adjust the quantities. It doesn't take any longer to cook."

Daniela's baked monkfish fillets

Clean the fish and carefully remove the skin. Cut the fish into 4–5 cm pieces. If it is too difficult with a knife, kitchen scissors are recommended. Preheat the oven to 180 °C.

Boil the potatoes in salted water for about 20 minutes. Then allow to cool briefly and cut them into pieces.

Place the fish pieces in an ovenproof pan lined with baking paper. Season with salt and pepper to taste.

Spread the potatoes and onions evenly over the fish. Pour the olive oil and white wine evenly over all the ingredients. Season with salt and pepper again, sprinkle with parsley and thyme.

Place the pan in the preheated oven. Cook on the middle shelf at 180 °C for about 15 minutes. Remove the pan from the oven, turn the fish and potatoes over and add the tomatoes. Then continue to bake for 5–10 minutes. Finish the dish with black olives and fresh herbs after baking.

Daniela recommends to use sharp kitchen scissors instead of a knife to cut the fish.

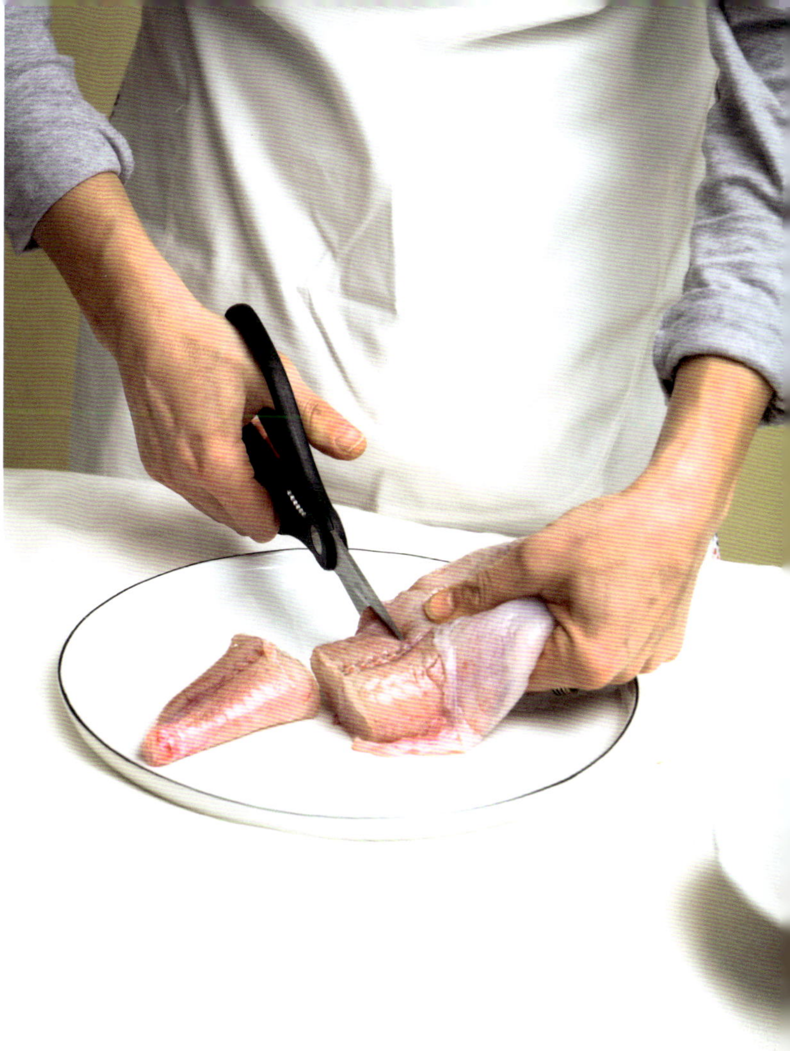

"If there is time, colleagues should always eat together at lunchtime."

Daniela is responsible for quality management at the Paul denim sewing shop, so she makes sure that the garments fit the way they should in the end. Not an easy job. But anyone can copy her baked monkfish fillets. "You don't need to be a master chef to make it," she says.

"The great thing about this dish is that you can make it in just one pan," says Daniela. Coda di rospo al forno means oven-baked monkfish. Cooked with potatoes, olives, garlic, tomatoes, parsley and a dash of white wine, it quickly becomes a light but flavoursome feast. "You don't need to be a master chef to make it."

Daniela works at Paul, a company that sews jeans for Closed. It is based in Ostra, a small town about 50 kilometres north-west of Ancona. Daniela started working in the firm's department for patterns and tailoring in 1988. Now, she is responsible for quality management, making sure the jeans fit and look the way they should when they are finished. "My job is similar to my colleague Onelia's (p. 88)," she says. This work demands a lot of concentration, which makes breaks all the more important. When there's enough time, the staff like to eat together. Everyone likes baked monkfish fillets.

"It's a good dish for anyone who isn't usually that keen on fish," says Daniela. "Or for people who are new to fish and want a gradual introduction." Monkfish flesh is firm and tastes more like crayfish. It has to be cut up to allow it to blend with the flavours of the other ingredients in the oven and, above all, absorb the sweetness and sharpness of the wine. Daniela uses sharp kitchen scissors to cut the fish. "That works best because monkfish have very strong spines." Next, she scatters parsley and garlic over the fish and mixes it with the other ingredients in the pan. Then the whole lot goes in the oven.

It doesn't really need any other side dishes but potatoes, browned until they are slightly crispy, complement it wonderfully. Fresh white bread completes the meal: perfect for dunking in the sauce made when the tomatoes, fish and wine are roasted in the oven.

Cheese, please!

Between Venice and Treviso lies the cheese dairy of Anna and her brother Riccardo. The speciality of Caseificio Artigiano Zanchetta: a mild-creamy cheese called Casatella.

"Casatella has to be creamy soft with a melt-in-the-mouth texture," says Anna, co-manager of artisan cheese company Caseificio Artigiano Zanchetta. A knife needs to be able to glide through a round with complete ease. This cows' milk cheese is typical of the Veneto region, and Anna's company has been making one of the best since 1972.

Caseificio Artigiano Zanchetta is halfway between Venice and Treviso in the small town of Casale sul Sale. About 13,000 people live here, amidst lots of green meadows and hills and a few ancient castle ruins. Anna's family business was established by her parents, Aurelio and Ilde. Now, she manages it with her brother Riccardo. They have 19 employees. A member of the next generation, Gilberto, is already waiting in the wings. "When we took over the business, it wasn't just about making a living. We wanted to continue our parents' work," says Anna.

The shop is testament to their success. Alongside regional cheese varieties like Casatella (which is relatively mild) and Montasio (which ranges from tangy to strong), the shop sells classic cows', sheep's, and goats' milk cheeses plus its own products like cream cheese dips, yoghurt, antipasti and fresh pasta. The sweet and savoury scent of fine foods hangs in the air. The counter is packed full of stock every morning, and it's nearly empty by evening. "Some people come here to buy food for the week; others pop in for a quick snack at lunchtime," says Anna. There are a few seats inside and outside the shop.

Back in the late 1990s, Anna and Riccardo launched a delivery service for customers who prefer to stay at home. "We've been delivering food every day since then – not just since the pandemic." It makes sense to offer this in the rural parts of northern Italy. Some villages don't have good transport links, and some people aren't able to walk far. Still, everyone should visit Caseificio Artigiano Zanchetta in person at least once in their lifetime.

Visitors can look through a little door behind the sales counter at the production area, where staff members wearing white coats and long blue gloves are usually busy at work, heating milk in large tubs and thickening it with rennet. After it has rested for long enough, they slice, cut and press it before storing the cheese until it reaches the required maturity. Each type of cheese has its own recipe, and the one for Casatella is very special indeed; it has been made since way back in the 17th century. Originally, the idea was to use up surplus milk in a way that would keep for a certain length of time, so almost every family in Veneto made their own Casatella with very simple equipment. Its name probably stems from the word "casada", which means "at home" in the local dialect. "This means that Casatella wasn't sold for a long time, and there are now dozens of variations on the recipe," says Anna. What makes her Casatella so creamy is, of course, a secret. She is completely open about the type of milk that's used to make it, though.

CASEIFICIO
Zanchetta

One of the two storage rooms at Caseificio Artigiano Zanchetta.

VECIA MASTEA
STAGIONATO
BASTARDO
MORLACCO
VECIA MASTEA
BASTARDO
MORLACCO
lemonsud

"We see it as our duty to produce everything locally." Anna and her brother Riccardo only work with nearby farmers who they know. "Within a radius of just a few kilometres, really. Some of them are smallholdings which don't have big herds. That means we can rest assured that the animals are treated well."

PARMIGIANO 189
REGGIANO
24 mesi
Grat. 191
20,80 €/Kg
Caseificio Artigiano Zanchetta

Dolci

There is always room for dessert – especially for homemade tiramisu, biscotti or panna cotta

Giovanna's tiramisu

Prep 30 min Cool 12 h Serves 6

300 ml espresso (or strong coffee)

120 g sugar

8 tbsp amaretto

5 egg yolks

A pinch of salt

750 g mascarpone

100 g whipped cream

250 g ladyfingers

Unsweetened cocoa powder

There are many stories about this dessert. The one about its origin goes like this: It is said to have been invented in 1969 at the restaurant Le Beccherie in Treviso. As well as coming up with the idea of soaking sponge cakes in coffee and spreading mascarpone over them, the owners invented the name of the dessert. Because the woman was pregnant, she needed a pick-me-up – which translates as "tira me sù". "The most important ingredient is patience," says Giovanna.

Make the espresso. Stir 4 tbsp sugar into the hot espresso until the sugar has dissolved completely. Allow to cool slightly. Add the amaretto to the warm espresso and stir. Set the espresso mixture aside.

Beat the egg yolks with the remaining sugar and salt for at least 2 minutes until thick and creamy. Briefly whisk mascarpone and 3 tbsp of the egg yolk mixture until smooth. Carefully fold in the remaining egg yolks spoon by spoon. Whip the cream until stiff and finally fold into the egg yolk and mascarpone mixture.

Briefly dip half of the ladyfingers individually into the cooled espresso mixture and place them next to each other in a baking dish (approx. 23 × 33 cm). Pour a little less than half of the mascarpone cream on top and smooth it down. Spread another layer of soaked ladyfingers on top and press down lightly. Pour the remaining mascarpone cream on top of the ladyfingers and smooth with a spoon – or decorate with peaks or waves.

Place in the fridge overnight. Just before serving, sift a generous amount of cocoa powder over the tiramisu.

Giovanna's tiramisu

"Working is much easier when there is good food."

Giovanna is responsible for creating the first sample pieces at shoe specialist Stil Tre. She likes to bring her colleagues something to eat. "My tiramisu is always a special treat for them. They all love it!" she says.

"When you cut it, none of the coffee should ooze out," says Giovanna, of the perfect tiramisu. Not even a drop of espresso; the ladyfingers must absorb it all yet stay firm.

Giovanna is an expert when it comes to tiramisu. She grew up with this dessert. "My mother always used to make it for me when there was something to celebrate or I did really well at school, or if I begged her long enough to," she says. Over the years, she learnt how to prepare it just by watching. The right proportion of ladyfingers to coffee, layering and soaking the sponge, and stirring the mixture of mascarpone and egg yolk. Now, Giovanna regularly makes tiramisu herself – sometimes for her colleagues Veronica (p. 184) or Paola (p. 138) when there is something to celebrate.

Giovanna works at Stil Tre. Located in an idyllic place called San Giovanni Ilarione between mountains and meadows east of Verona, this producer makes footwear for Closed. Giovanna started work at the sales department there when she was 20. "The job was pretty much on my doorstep. It was a perfect fit," she says.

Now, almost 13 years later, she takes care of samples. This means she is responsible for designing and producing prototypes, and liaising with clients and the manufacturing team at Stil Tre. "Sometimes it's pretty stressful, but I love that. Adrenaline is part and parcel of achieving a good finished product."

The same applies to the perfect tiramisu. Only at the very end does it become clear whether the consistency is right. It is also essential that none of the ingredients are left out. "You have to be patient," says Giovanna. "A good tiramisu needs to rest in a cool place overnight or even longer."

Lidia and Luca's spumini

Prep 15 min   Bake 2 h   For 30 spumini

3 egg whites

1 pinch of salt

200 g sugar

1 tsp lemon juice

Dark chocolate to taste, grated

Spumini is a type of meringue – whipped egg whites baked in the oven with sugar, a pinch of salt and lemon juice. Their distinctive feature is their size. "Spumini should be gone in a bite or two," says Lidia.

Preheat the oven to 100 °C. Beat the egg whites and salt until stiff. Slowly add the sugar and lemon juice. Continue beating until the sugar has completely dissolved. Place about 30 small egg white puffs on a baking sheet lined with baking paper.

Dry the meringue in the preheated oven at 100 °C for about 2 hours with the oven door slightly open. It is best to place a wooden spoon in the oven door.

Switch the oven off and leave the spumini to cool in the oven. Sprinkle freshly grated chocolate flakes over the cooled spumini as desired.

Giada's mantovana

Prep 15 min Bake 30 min For 12 pieces

1 egg

4 egg yolks

170 g sugar

Pinch of salt

170 g flour

150 g butter, melted

The zest of 1 organic lemon

120 g almonds, roughly chopped

Icing sugar to finish

No one knows why this Tuscan speciality is named after the city of Mantua, which is in Lombardy. The most credible theory is that some nuns from Mantua gave the recipe to Pellegrino Artusi, a merchant, gourmet and the founder of Italian national cuisine, who then took it to Prato. One thing is for sure, though: "When baked, this cake doesn't rise but it becomes really soft," says Giada.

Beat the egg and egg yolks with sugar and a pinch of salt in a bowl until foamy. Gradually add the flour. Stir in the butter and lemon zest.

Preheat the oven to 170 °C. Meanwhile, grease a round baking tin (24 cm) with butter and dust with a little flour.

Pour the mixture into the tin and move it slightly to distribute it evenly. Sprinkle the surface with the chopped almonds. Bake the cake in a preheated oven at 170 °C for about 30 minutes.

Remove the finished cake from the oven and let it cool completely. Dust with icing sugar before serving.

"It is important to preserve and pass on old family recipes."

Giada creates the sample collections at the knitwear manufacturer Pooltrend. "When something then goes into serial production, I know from start to finish how it was made and has to be made," she says. She also knows every recipe detail of a mantovana by heart. "On Sundays and whenever the family got together, that's how we had it when I was a little girl."

"What makes a mantovana so special is the fact that it doesn't rise when it's baked but it's still really soft," says Giada. She knows this almond cake recipe inside out. "We always used to eat this on Sundays and whenever the whole family got together." She doesn't need an excuse to bake it these days either.

The cake is very easy to prepare, making it ideal for beginner bakers. Giada has some tips for those who are just starting out: "I make sure the tin is greased well beforehand and dusted with flour. That makes it easier to remove the cake afterwards." Then, she whisks eggs, sugar and salt until the mixture is frothy, stirs in the flour, and adds melted butter and lemon zest. She puts it all in a cake tin and scatters almonds on the top. That's the bulk of the work done.

Giada has worked at Pooltrend since 2015. The company makes products such as scarves and blankets for Closed. Located in the town of Montemurlo, which belongs to the province of Prato, it has long been in demand internationally for its expertise in knitted accessories.

Giada is responsible for sample collections and individual samples, which means prototypes of designs which have not yet gone into serial production. "Lots of our partners add their own details to our designs," she says. Giada oversees this process from start to finish. "When something goes into production, I know how it was made and has to be made." It's the same with baking.

Giada knows exactly how long a mantovana should remain in the oven. Although the recipe says approximately 30 minutes, it is just right when a toothpick inserted into the cake comes out clean. Then she leaves it to cool before dusting it with icing sugar. "Mantovana tastes best fresh from the oven, but you can keep it for a few days."

Beatrice's maritozzi

Prep 30 min Rest/bake 1 h 15 min Makes 12

500 g flour

100 g sugar

Pinch of salt

1 cube of yeast

120 ml milk, lukewarm

100 ml neutral vegetable oil

2 eggs + 1 egg yolk

The zest of 1 organic orange

150 g raisins (optional)

250 ml whipped cream for the filling (optional)

1 sachet bourbon vanilla sugar for the filling (optional)

Icing sugar to finish

The name maritozzi comes from the Italian word for husband, "marito". The brioche-style rolls were given this name because they used to serve as a declaration of love in Rome, where they originate from. They were originally only made during Lent, when husbands gave them to their wives every Friday in March. Nowadays, maritozzi are eaten throughout Italy all year round. "They look great at any party buffet," says Beatrice.

In a large bowl, mix the flour, sugar and salt. Make a well in the centre. Mix the yeast and 5 tbsp lukewarm milk until the yeast has completely liquefied. Pour the yeast mixture into the flour well and mix with a little flour from the edge. Cover the preferment with a tea towel and leave to rise in a warm place for about 15 minutes.

Add the oil, two eggs, orange zest, remaining milk and raisins to the preferment. Knead first with the dough hook of a hand mixer, then by hand, to a smooth dough. Cover the dough and let it rise for 45–60 minutes until it has doubled in volume.

Preheat the oven to 200 °C. Knead the dough again. Shape into 12 round rolls.

Place the rolls on a baking sheet lined with baking paper and leave to rest for 5–10 minutes. Mix the egg yolk and 1 tbsp milk and brush the rolls with the mixture. Bake in the preheated oven for approx. 15 minutes.

For the optional cream filling: whip the cream with the vanilla sugar and a pinch of salt. Cut the maritozzi in half and fill them with cream. Dust with icing sugar before serving.

“With fashion and food, it’s all about the details. Everything has to be perfect.”

Beatrice is an expert in belt loops and buttons at the denim sewing shop Paul. She has learned the craft over the years. “With the maritozzi, it’s also the little things that matter a lot,” she says. “The milk mustn’t be too hot and you mustn’t use too much flour.”

"We used to bake maritozzi when I was little," says Beatrice. These little brioche-style rolls, with or without raisins, have always been a popular dessert in her family. They also make a great mid-afternoon snack. "It's easy to make a big batch of maritozzi and keep them for a few days."

Beatrice has worked at Paul since 2004. Jeans for Closed have been sewn there for over 40 years. The company is based in Ostra, a small town about 50 kilometres north-west of Ancona. Beatrice specialises in belt loops and buttons. "I attach them by hand and with a punching machine," she says. It is extremely precise work. Even the tiniest inaccuracy makes a product faulty. "The same is true of maritozzi." There are two crucial things to remember when preparing this recipe. Firstly, the milk in which the yeast is dissolved mustn't be too hot. If it is, the yeast won't rise later on.

To make sure the temperature is right, Beatrice dips a finger in the milk and puts it on her upper lip. If it feels nice and warm, it's time to move on to the next step in the recipe. Secondly, the dough mustn't be sticky as that also stops the yeast from rising. "Therefore, you mustn't add too little or too much flour."

It takes a bit of practice to get maritozzi right, but fresh from the oven, steaming and warm, they make a delicious sweet treat. "You can cut them and spread them too," adds Beatrice. "With mascarpone or chocolate spread, cream or jam. That's what I used to do as a child."

Alessandra and Carla's panna cotta

Prep 25 min Cool 5 h Serves 4

8 g gelatine

500 ml whipping cream

1 vanilla pod

80 g sugar

250 g strawberries, halved

This cream dessert is considered traditional in the northern Italian region of Piedmont. A dictionary from 1879 mentions a dish called latte inglese, which consists of cream cooked and moulded with gelatine. The term panna cotta, however, did not appear in Italian cookbooks until the 1960s. "Chilled, it is perfect on a hot summer's day," says Alessandra.

Soak the gelatine in cold water for 10–15 minutes. Pour the cream into a small saucepan. Scrape out the vanilla pod.

Add the vanilla seeds (out of the pod), the empty pod and the sugar to the cream and heat at a low temperature. As soon as the cream starts to boil, remove the pan from the heat. Remove the vanilla pod.

Squeeze the soaked gelatine to remove excess water. Add to the hot cream and stir until the gelatine has completely dissolved and no lumps remain. Divide into four equal-sized ramekins and place in the fridge for at least 5 hours.

Before serving, dip the ramekins briefly in hot water to make the panna cotta easier to turn out. Serve with strawberries.

Alessandra and Carla's panna cotta

Monia's biscotti di Prato

Prep 30 min Rest / bake 1 h Makes 35 biscotti

270 g flour

150 g sugar

100 g pine nuts, ground or crushed with a pestle and mortar

180 g almonds (unpeeled)

Salt

2 eggs, beaten
(optional: 1 egg yolk for coating)

30 g butter

Biscotto comes from the Latin "biscoctus" and means "baked twice". People used to put the almond biscuits in the oven twice so that they would keep well, for example for a long journey. Now, it is mainly done to achieve a consistency which is both crumbly and firm. "In keeping with the tradition, you dip them in a glass of Vin Santo!" says Monia.

Put the flour, sugar, ground pine nuts, almonds and a pinch of salt in a bowl. Add the eggs, butter and 6–8 tbsp water and knead well until an even dough is formed. It should be compact but still malleable. Leave the dough to rest in the fridge for 30 minutes.

Preheat the oven to 200 °C. Divide the dough into four and form long rolls (approx. 3 cm wide) on a floured work surface. Brush with egg yolk if desired.

Place the rolls with enough space between them (at least 5 cm) on a baking tray lined with baking paper and flatten slightly. Bake the biscotti in the oven at 200 °C for 20 minutes on the middle shelf.

Leave to cool the rolls slightly. Cut diagonally into slices approx. 1 cm wide with a sharp knife. Place them individually on the baking tray again for the optional second baking process (15 minutes), which Monia waives.

"The path to success leads through the kitchen, even at work."

Monia works in the export department of the yarn manufacturer Pecci Filati and makes sure that goods always reach the clients on time. Monia's biscotti di Prato are very popular with them. "The dessert is ideal for larger groups of people coming together around a table," she says.

Most people know these crumbly and crunchy almond biscuits by the name of cantuccini and have come across them served with coffee. However, they originate from the province of Prato, near Florence, whey they usually go by a different name. "Biscotti di Prato," says Monia – in other words, biscuits from Prato.

Monia was born in Prato and still lives there. She works at Pecci Filati. The company produces high-quality yarns, such as wool and cotton yarns for Closed knitwear. It is located in Campi Bisenzio, halfway between Prato and Florence. Monia works in the export department and is responsible for liaising with haulage companies to make sure that goods are always delivered to clients safely and on time. She has been doing this job since 2014.

She grew up with biscotti di Prato. "They're typical of this region and an integral part of our culture," she says. The recipe has been handed down from generation to generation in her family. It involves stirring ground pine nuts into a biscuit mixture of flour and sugar, which gives the finished biscotti a finer flavour. "It's very important to stir all the ingredients together well to make an even mixture," says Monia. "There's no harm in leaving the dough to rest for a few hours as well."

Afterwards, the almonds are stirred in and the dough is made into evenly shaped rolls with a maximum diameter of three centimetres. They will rise slightly in the oven. "That's why you should leave some space between them on the baking sheet," Monia adds. When they come out of the oven, the rolls need to cool slightly before they are sliced.

Traditionally, biscotti di Prato are not served with coffee. Instead, they accompany a dessert wine called Vin Santo, which also originates from Tuscany. Made from air-dried, partially desiccated grapes, it has subtle notes of apricot and amaretto.

"You pour yourself a small glass and dunk the biscotti in it," says Monia, until they are saturated and soft. The result is both tangy and sweet. "I recommend breaking with tradition and only baking the biscuits once so they don't get too hard. They taste just as good!"

Dolce vita

Cakes and pastries, and in the hands of a family for four generations: Luca and his father Milo's Pasticceria Luisita on Lake Como.

There used to be dozens of cake shops around Lake Como. Now, there are scarcely a handful of bakeries that use old, original recipes. One of them is Pasticceria Luisita, which has a shop in the historic part of Como and its main building a bit further away from the centre in Via Luigi Dottesio.

Behind the counter (which is jam-packed with cannoli, cornetti, pasticciotti and ice cream) are the senior and junior managers of this family business, Milo and Luca. Luca joined about ten years ago and represents the fourth generation to work there. "Luisita was my great-grandmother," he explains. "Her family came from Italy, but they emigrated to Buenos Aires, where she was born. Hence the name." When she returned to Italy, Luisita made a living by selling milk and butter. "That was in 1921, right here where our shop is now." Since then, each generation has made its own contribution to the development of Pasticceria Luisita. Luca's grandfather started making meringues and ice cream. "He even built his own manufacturing machine using motorbike parts." Luca's father and his uncle Maurizio focused on cakes and pastries.

Luca wasn't passionate about baking at first. "I studied design and communication," he says. When he graduated, he initially went freelance. "But then my father asked me whether I could help him with the invoices. On my first day, I worked for two hours. The next day, I did twelve." Luca has been taking care of the business side of things ever since. If asked nicely, he might just take visitors to see the production facility, which is a stone's throw from the shop.

Five pastry cooks knead, shape, ice and decorate sweet treats there six days a week. "I call them artists," says Luca. They have perfected every aspect of confectionery, like filling tortelli with sweet cream. These little pastry balls are deep-fried then rolled in sugar, and have a similar consistency to doughnuts (but with a thicker crust). They are traditionally eaten during the carnival season, but Pasticceria Luisita doesn't just sell them then. "That's what our customers want," says Luca.

Rocco has been a pastry chef at
Pasticceria Luisita for many years.

TORTE LUISITA
ZUCCOTTI
SPUMONI

Speciality of the house:
cannoli filled with cream.

One of the shop's specialities is a cake called la resta di Como. The recipe was invented in the early 19th century – not long before the shop first opened – in a taverna. Its owner wanted to make a cake with dried fruit for a group of fishermen, but he used too much yeast. He kept the overflowing cake mixture in check while it was baking by putting a stick in it and twisting it repeatedly to hold everything together. The finished result was a dome-shaped cake which is still made today with a stick inside it and decorated with a herringbone pattern in memory of the fishermen. Luca says: "The cake resulted from a mistake, but the best things often come about that way."

The men behind the counter: Luca (left) and his father Milo (right).

Founder and namesake of the pasticceria: Luisita.

SALUMÍ
Levoni
GUSTA LA DIFFERENZA
NORSCIA
PREMIUM
BIRRA
BEER
Nastro
Azzurro

Dennis Braatz

Dennis Braatz, author and journalist, writes for publications such as Welt am Sonntag, Icon, Vogue, Stern, and Süddeutsche Zeitung. He lives in Munich.

Roselena Ramistella

Roselena Ramistella, photographer and political scientist, works for publications such as Vogue, La Repubblica, and The Guardian. She lives in Sicily.

Shanti (left) and Maria (right) making pasta dough (p. 100) on a folding.

The promenade in the city of Como on Lake Como.

Oro della Terra
Oro della Terra

Grazie!

Thank you, Alessandra, Carla, Giulio, Enrico, Luana, Carlo, Claudia, Shanti, Maria, Silvia, Andrea, Rosanna, Giovanni, Antonio, Claudio, Lidia, Luca M., Onelia, Alessandro, Sara, Alberto, Barbara, Elena, Paola, Maurizio, Fabrizio, Stella, Lorenzo, Veronica, Marco, Daniela, Anna, Aurelio, Gilberto, Giovanna, Giada, Beatrice, Monia, Milo, Luca C. and Rocco, for your hospitality and patience.

You are always welcome to visit!

Imprint

Cucina Closed – A cookbook featuring our Italian manufacturers and their family recipes

Edited by Gordon Giers

Concept: Hjördis Pflughaupt

Photography: Roselena Ramistella

Text: Dennis Braatz

Food Styling: Katja Baum

Editorial Management: Laura Reinke

Recipe Texts: Ann-Marie Galazka

Design and Layout: Sina Harrsen, Nils Reinke-Dieker

Typefaces: Brown LL and Lyon Text

Project Management gestalten: Lars Pietzschmann

Project Management Closed: Lisa Jena, Jennifer Samel

Photography Assistance: Eugenio Chen

Retouch: Claudio Palmisano

Production: Nik Jesih

Support: Anna Marleen Kutsch, Minou Sheidany, Giulia Stanzione und Nora Wallersheim

Translation/Proofreading Textra Fachübersetzungen

Closed GmbH
Straßenbahnring 6
20251 Hamburg

Exclusively distributed by:
Die Gestalten Verlag GmbH & Co. KG
www.gestalten.com

Printed by Gutenberg Beuys Feindruckerei GmbH, Langenhagen

Made in Germany

ISBN 978-3-96704-116-3

For more information, and to order books, please visit www.gestalten.com

Bibliographic information published by the Deutsche Nationalbibliothek. The Deutsche Nationalbibliothek lists this publication in the Deutsche Nationalbibliografie; detailed bibliographic data is available online at www.dnb.de

This book was printed on paper certified according to the standards of the FSC®.

FSC www.fsc.org MIX Paper from responsible sources FSC® C009051